Sonship

A Kingdom of Sons

Tom Cornell

SONSHIP

A KINGDOM OF SONS

TOM CORNELL

SOZO PUBLISHING

CONTENTS

INTRODUCTION
THE CRY OF SONSHIP

Adam walked with God in the cool of the day. He had no fear, no shame, and no striving. He was simply a son, created in the image of his Father, living from love and communion. He was not a servant trying to earn favor. He was not an orphan searching for a home. He was a son who belonged. But when sin entered the world, something was lost—sonship was exchanged for separation.

From that moment, humanity began to live outside of its original design. Adam, once called the son of God (Luke 3:38), became disconnected from the source of life. Mankind no longer knew who they were. They became slaves to fear, striving to earn approval from a distant God, wandering in an orphan mindset.

But the Father never stopped longing for His children to come home. Jesus came to restore what was lost.

"For the Son of Man has come to seek and to save that which was lost." – Luke 19:10 NKJV

Jesus did not just come to rescue us from sin. He came to restore us to our identity. He is called the Son of Man not just because He was fully human, but because He came to show us what humanity was meant to be. He walked in perfect relationship with the Father, living in total dependence and love. Everything He did—healing the sick, raising the dead, loving the broken—flowed from one truth:

"the Son can do nothing of Himself, but what He sees the Father do"
– John 5:19 NKJV

This is the foundation of sonship. Sons and daughters do not strive; they receive. They do not perform; they abide. Jesus never lived from pressure or insecurity—He lived from the Father's voice and love. He came so that we could do the same.

The Orphan Spirit vs. Sonship

The enemy has worked tirelessly to keep believers trapped in an orphan spirit—living like spiritual beggars instead of beloved children. An orphan spirit says:

- I must earn love and approval.
- I don't have access to my inheritance.
- I am alone and have to fight for myself.
- I am a servant, not a son.

But Jesus came to break this mindset and bring us back to the Father's heart. The Gospel is not just about forgiveness—it is about adoption.

"For you did not receive the spirit of bondage again to fear, but you received the Spirit of adoption by whom we cry out, "Abba, Father."
– Romans 8:15 NKJV

This is why the earth is groaning for the revealing of true sons (Romans 8:19). The world is not waiting for more religious people. It is not waiting for more church goers. It is waiting for sons and daughters who know who they are and walk in the authority, love, and power of the Kingdom. The Government of God Rests on Sons The Father did not send a servant to restore the world. He sent a Son. Isaiah prophesied of Jesus:

> *"For unto us a Child is born, Unto us a Son is given; And the government will be upon His shoulder." - Isaiah 9:6 NKJV*

God's government—His Kingdom, authority, and dominion —is always entrusted to sons. A child is born, but a son is given. Children are loved, but sons are entrusted. This means that spiritual maturity is required for us to carry Kingdom authority. The Father is looking for sons and daughters who will take responsibility for bringing His Kingdom to earth—just as Jesus did.

Your Journey into Sonship

This book is an invitation to step into your true identity. It is a call to break free from the orphan spirit and embrace your place in the Father's house. As you read, you will learn:

- How to shift from an orphan mindset to sonship
- How to walk in the Father's love and intimacy
- How to access your inheritance and authority
- How to bring heaven to earth as a mature son or daughter

> *Jesus said, "He who has seen Me has seen the Father" - John 14:9 NKJV*

This means that everything He did—His compassion, His

miracles, His words—revealed the nature of the Father. You were created for the same purpose. The world will see the Father through you when you step into sonship. It's time to come home. It's time to live as a son.

1

UNDERSTANDING THE ORPHAN SPIRIT

Adam was created as a son of God (Luke 3:38). He was designed to walk in perfect relationship with the Father, living from love, not fear. But when sin entered the world, something deeper than just disobedience happened—sonship was broken. Adam and Eve hid from God, fear replaced intimacy, and for the first time, humanity felt separated.

Since that moment, mankind has been living under what many call the orphan spirit—a deep, internal belief that we are fatherless, abandoned, or unworthy of true love. This orphan mindset is one of the greatest barriers to fully embracing the Kingdom of God. It keeps us striving, fearing, and trying to prove ourselves rather than simply receiving the Father's love as sons and daughters.

But here's the truth: Jesus came to restore what was lost.

"For the Son of Man came to seek and to save the lost."
– Luke 19:10 ESV

Jesus didn't just come to save us from hell; He came to bring us home. He came to break the orphan spirit and restore us to the Father's embrace.

What is the Orphan Spirit?

The orphan spirit is not just a psychological condition—it is a spiritual condition that affects how we relate to God, ourselves, and others. It is a mindset that causes people to feel:

- Rejected instead of accepted
- Fearful instead of secure
- Striving instead of resting
- Performance-driven instead of love-driven

The orphan spirit causes believers to serve God rather than walk with Him as sons. It makes people see God as a distant Master instead of a loving Father.

> *"You did not receive a spirit of slavery to fall back into fear, but you received the Spirit of adoption as sons, by whom we cry, 'Abba! Father!'"* – Romans 8:15 ESV

Paul tells us that we have been adopted, but many still live as slaves. If we do not know who we are, we will never live as sons and daughters—we will continue to strive, struggle, and live below our inheritance.

The First Orphan: How Satan Lost Sonship

The first being to experience an orphan mindset was not Adam —it was Satan himself. Originally, Lucifer was an angel of light, created by God, given authority in heaven. But something changed:

> *"You said in your heart, I will ascend to heaven; above the stars of*

God I will set my throne on high... I will make myself like the Most High.'"– Isaiah 14:13-14 ESV

Satan wanted position without relationship. He wanted authority without sonship. He rejected submission to the Father and, in doing so, lost his place in heaven. When Satan tempted Eve in the garden, his strategy was the same—he planted the seed of orphan thinking:

"For God knows that when you eat from it your eyes will be opened, and you will be like God, knowing good and evil." – Genesis 3:5 NIV

This is a lie. Adam and Eve were already like God—they were made in His image! But the orphan spirit convinces people that they must earn what they already have. When Adam and Eve fell into this trap, they lost their sonship. They immediately felt naked, ashamed, and afraid.

"Then the man and his wife heard the sound of the LORD God as he was walking in the garden in the cool of the day, and they hid from the LORD God among the trees of the garden." – Genesis 3:8 NIV

This is what orphans do—they hide. They do not believe they are worthy of love, so they try to cover themselves with their own efforts. But the Father was still looking for His sons.

The Symptoms of an Orphan Spirit

Many believers today love Jesus, but they still live with an orphan mentality. They struggle with:

1. Fear and Anxiety

- Orphans feel unprotected and alone
- Sons rest in the Father's care (Matthew 6:26)

2. Performance and Striving

- Orphans try to earn God's love
- Sons know they are already accepted (Ephesians 1:5)

3. Insecurity and Jealousy

- Orphans compare themselves to others
- Sons celebrate the Father's goodness in their lives (Luke 15:31)

4. Lack of Intimacy with the Father

- Orphans feel like God is distant
- Sons live in constant relationship (John 14:9)

Many people in the Church today act like the older brother in the parable of the Prodigal Son. They are obedient, but they do not know how to receive the Father's love.

"All these years I've been slaving for you and never disobeyed your orders... but you never gave me even a young goat so I could celebrate with my friends." – Luke 15:29 NIV

He was living in the Father's house, but he had the heart of an orphan.

Jesus Came to Restore Sonship

The Father did not send a servant to fix the problem of sin. He sent a Son.

"For to us a child is born, to us a son is given, and the government will be on his shoulders." – Isaiah 9:6 NIV

Jesus came to restore us to sonship. He modeled what a true son looks like:

- He lived in perfect relationship with the Father
- He walked in authority and confidence
- He never acted independently—He did only what the Father showed Him (John 5:19)

This is why Jesus was called the Son of Man—He came to reveal what mankind was supposed to look like.

Jesus said, "He who has seen Me has seen the Father" – John 14:9 NKJV

Jesus came to show us the Father's love. He came to bring us home.

The Earth is Crying Out for Sons

Paul tells us that all of creation is waiting for something:

"For the creation waits in eager expectation for the children of God to be revealed." – Romans 8:19 NIV

The world does not need more religious people—it needs sons and daughters who walk in their identity. It is time for the Church to break free from an orphan spirit and step into the full inheritance of the Kingdom.

You Were Created for Sonship

If you are in Christ, you are not an orphan. You are a son, a daughter, an heir. The Father is calling you home—not just to heaven, but to relationship.

"Everything I have is yours." – Luke 15:31 NKJV

No more striving. No more fear. It's time to live as a son.

Activation Prayer

Father, I repent for living with an orphan mindset. I renounce the lie that I have to earn Your love. I receive my identity as Your child. I declare that I am adopted, accepted, and loved. Holy Spirit, reveal the Father's love to me. I choose to live as a son, not a slave. Amen.

Discussion Questions

1 . In what ways have you personally identified with the orphan spirit described in this chapter—such as striving, fear, or feeling distant from God? How does recognizing this mindset help you receive the Father's love more fully?

2 . Why do you think Satan's strategy in the garden was to plant a seed of orphan thinking, rather than simply tempt with disobedience? What does this reveal about the power of identity in spiritual warfare?

3 . Romans 8:19 says creation is waiting for the sons of God to be revealed. What might it look like for you to walk in your identity as a son or daughter of God in your daily life, family, or calling?

2
THE FATHER'S HEART FOR HIS CHILDREN

From the very beginning, God has desired one thing: relationship with His children. He is not looking for religious servants—He is looking for sons and daughters who know Him intimately. The entire story of Scripture, from Genesis to Revelation, is a story of a Father longing to bring His children home.

"See what great love the Father has lavished on us, that we should be called children of God! And that is what we are!" – 1 John 3:1 NIV

Many believers struggle with seeing God as Father because they have only known Him as a distant ruler or an impersonal force. But Jesus came to change that perception. He came to reveal the Father and to restore us to the intimacy we were always meant to have.

Jesus Came to Reveal the Father

One of Jesus' greatest missions was to introduce humanity to the Father. Before Jesus, people knew God as Elohim (Creator), Yahweh (Lord), and Jehovah (Provider, Healer, and Ruler). But very few people understood God as Father. That is why Jesus' teachings were so revolutionary. He constantly referred to God as "My Father" and invited us to do the same.

"If you have seen me, you have seen the Father." – John 14:9 NIV

This statement changed everything. Jesus was saying, "Look at me, and you will see what the Father is like." The love, compassion, patience, and kindness of Jesus were not just His personality —they were a direct reflection of the Father's heart. Everything Jesus did—healing the sick, forgiving the broken, feeding the hungry—was an expression of the Father's nature.

"the Son can do nothing by himself. He does only what he sees the Father doing." – John 5:19 NLT

Jesus did not operate independently. He lived in constant intimacy with the Father, showing us how sons and daughters are meant to live.

The Father's Heart in the Parable of the Prodigal Son

One of the most powerful pictures of the Father's heart is found in Luke 15:11-32—the parable of the prodigal son.

The Younger Son: Rebellion and Return

The younger son represents those who have walked away from the Father. He demanded his inheritance early, left home, and wasted it all on reckless living. He ended up in poverty, shame, and regret, believing he could never return home. But the moment he decided to return, something incredible happened:

"While he was still a long way off, his father saw him and was

filled with compassion for him; he ran to his son, threw his arms
around him and kissed him." – Luke 15:20 NIV

This was unheard of in Jewish culture. Fathers did not run—
especially not toward a rebellious, shameful son. But this Father
ran. He embraced. He restored.

This is the Father's heart for every lost son and daughter. He
is not standing with arms crossed, waiting to punish you—He is
running toward you with open arms.

The Older Brother: The Orphan Mentality in the Church

But there was another son in the story—the older brother. He
never left home, but he also never knew the Father's heart. When
the younger son was welcomed back, the older brother became
angry and jealous:

"All these years I've been slaving for you and never disobeyed your
orders... But when this son of yours comes home, you kill the fattened
calf for him!" – Luke 15:29 NIV

The older brother saw himself as a servant, not a son. He
believed his hard work should earn him more than the younger
brother. But the Father responded with tenderness:

"My son, you are always with me, and everything I have is yours." –
Luke 15:31 NIV

This is the heart of the Father. He longs for all His children to
know that they do not have to strive, beg, or compete— everything He has already belongs to us.

The Difference Between a Servant and a Son

Many Christians today are living like the older brother—working hard for God but never experiencing the joy of sonship.

Here's the difference between a servant and a son:

Servants	Sons
Work for approval	Work from approval
Feels distant from God	Feels intimate with the Father
Lives by rules	Lives by relationship
Strives to earn love	Receives love freely

Jesus came so that we would no longer be servants, but sons.

"I no longer call you servants, because a servant does not know his master's business. Instead, I have called you friends." – John 15:15 NIV

The Spirit of Sonship vs. The Orphan Spirit

Paul explains that when we receive Christ, we receive the Spirit of Sonship:

"You have not received a spirit of slavery leading to fear, but you have received a spirit of adoption as sons, by whom we cry out, 'Abba! Father!'" – Romans 8:15 NASB

An orphan spirit makes people:

- Feel unworthy of love
- Struggle with fear and rejection
- Live as though they must earn approval

But the Spirit of Sonship brings:

- Confidence in God's love
- Freedom from striving

- A deep sense of belonging

The Holy Spirit is the Spirit of Adoption—He helps us experience the Father's love and live as sons and daughters.

How to Experience the Father's Love

Many believers know in their heads that God is a Father, but they have not experienced His love in their hearts. How can we move from knowing to experiencing?

1. Ask the Holy Spirit to Reveal the Father's Love

The Holy Spirit is the One who makes the Father real to us.

"The Spirit Himself testifies with our spirit that we are children of God." – Romans 8:16 NASB

Ask Him: "Holy Spirit, show me the Father's love."

2. Spend Time in the Father's Presence

Jesus spent hours in prayer because He loved being with His Father. Sonship is built on intimacy.

"But Jesus often withdrew to lonely places and prayed." – Luke 5:16 NIV

3. Meditate on the Word of God

The Bible is full of promises about your identity. Read them, declare them, and let them change your thinking.

4. Surrender Your Orphan Mindset

Ask God to heal any area where you have believed the lie that you are an orphan. Say, "Father, I choose to believe I am fully loved, fully accepted, and fully Yours."

The Father's Invitation

The Father is calling you into deeper intimacy. He is saying: "Everything I have is yours. Come home." No more fear. No more striving. No more living as a servant. You are a son, a daughter, and an heir.

Activation Prayer

Father, I receive Your love today. I renounce the orphan spirit and embrace my identity as Your child. Holy Spirit, reveal the Father's heart to me. Let me experience His love in a deeper way. I choose to live as a son, not a servant. Amen.

Discussion Questions

1 . Why do you think so many believers relate more to God as a distant ruler than as a loving Father? How did Jesus' life and words confront that perception?

2 . In the parable of the prodigal son, how do the responses of the younger and older brothers reflect different struggles with identity? Which one do you relate to more right now—and why?

3 . What does it practically look like to "live as a son and not a servant" in your relationship with God? How can you intentionally grow in intimacy with the Father this week?

3

THE PRODIGAL AND THE OLDER BROTHER
TWO SIDES OF THE SAME ORPHAN MENTALITY

One of the greatest parables Jesus told about sonship is the story of the Prodigal Son in Luke 15:11-32. This story is not just about a wayward son returning home—it is about the heart of the Father, and how both rebellion and religion can keep us from fully embracing our identity as sons and daughters.

Many believers today still struggle with the orphan spirit—whether they are like the younger son, running from God, or like the older son, striving to earn His love. This chapter will explore how both sons had an orphan mindset and how the Father's response reveals God's heart for His children.

The Younger Son – Rebellion and Return

Jesus begins the story with a shocking statement:

"There was a man who had two sons. The younger one said to his father, 'Father, give me my share of the estate.' So he divided his property between them." – Luke 15:11-12 NIV

In Jewish culture, this was an unthinkable request. To ask for an inheritance while the father was still alive was essentially saying: "I wish you were dead." It was the ultimate rejection of relationship in favor of independence and self-will. The younger son left home and squandered everything on reckless living. But when famine struck, he found himself destitute, hungry, and abandoned.

"So he went and hired himself out to a citizen of that country, who sent him to his fields to feed pigs. He longed to fill his stomach with the pods that the pigs were eating, but no one gave him anything." – Luke 15:15-16 NIV

This was rock bottom. Feeding pigs was one of the lowest jobs for a Jewish man—it symbolized complete uncleanness and separation from his heritage.

The Lie of the Orphan Spirit – "I Am Not Worthy"

Then something happened:

"When he came to his senses, he said, 'How many of my father's hired servants have food to spare, and here I am starving to death! I will set out and go back to my father and say to him: Father, I have sinned against heaven and against you. I am no longer worthy to be called your son; make me like one of your hired servants.'" – Luke 15:17-19 NIV

Here we see the orphan mindset in action. The son recognized his failure, but instead of believing he could be restored as a son, he only hoped to be accepted as a servant.

This is what the orphan spirit does—it convinces us that we are not worthy of love and that we must earn our place in the Father's house.

The Father's Radical Response – Restoration, Not Rejection

The younger son expected rejection. He expected to have to prove himself. But the Father had a completely different response:

"But while he was still a long way off, his father saw him and was filled with compassion for him; he ran to his son, threw his arms around him and kissed him." – Luke 15:20 NIV

This verse reveals so much about the Father's heart:

- The Father was watching—He never stopped looking for His son.
- The Father ran—which was undignified for a Jewish patriarch.
- The Father embraced him before he could explain himself—love was given freely.

Before the son could even finish his speech, the Father interrupted him and commanded immediate restoration:

"Quick! Bring the best robe and put it on him. Put a ring on his finger and sandals on his feet." – Luke 15:22 NIV

Each of these symbols is significant:

- The robe – A covering of honor and identity (Isaiah 61:10).
- The ring – A symbol of authority and family inheritance.
- The sandals – A sign of sonship (servants went barefoot).

Key Truth: Sonship is Restored Instantly

The Father didn't make him work his way back into the family. He didn't demand proof of repentance. He immediately restored him as a son, not a servant. This is how God restores every lost son and daughter who returns to Him.

The Older Brother – The Orphan Spirit in Religion

But the story doesn't end there. The older brother had been faithfully serving in his father's house, yet when he heard that his lost brother had been welcomed back, he became angry:

"The older brother became angry and refused to go in. So his father went out and pleaded with him." – Luke 15:28 NIV

Instead of rejoicing over his brother's return, he was offended. He felt like he had worked harder and deserved more:

"All these years I've been slaving for you and never disobeyed your orders, yet you never gave me even a young goat so I could celebrate with my friends." – Luke 15:29 NIV

The Lie of the Orphan Spirit – "I Must Earn Love"

The older brother saw himself as a servant, not a son. He thought that his obedience and hard work should earn him more favor. But the Father responded with love and truth:

"My son, you are always with me, and everything I have is yours." – Luke 15:31 NIV

This verse reveals a key truth: Many believers are living in the Father's house but still have an orphan mindset.

The Two Orphan Mentalities

The Younger Son (Rebellion)	The Older Brother (Religion)
Runs from God	Works for God
Feels unworthy	Feels entitled
Lives in shame	Lives in pride
Believes they must beg for forgiveness	Believes they must earn favor
Sees God as a Master	Sees God as an Employer

Both sons misunderstood the Father's love. One thought he had lost sonship, the other thought he had to earn sonship.

But the truth is: Sonship is given, not earned.

"You have not received a spirit of slavery leading to fear, but you have received the Spirit of adoption as sons." – Romans 8:15 NASB

The Father's Invitation – Come Home as a Son

The younger son needed to return to the Father's love. The older son needed to receive the Father's love. The Father is calling both rebels and religious people to come home—not as servants, but as sons and daughters.

"For the creation waits in eager expectation for the children of God to be revealed." – Romans 8:19 NIV

The world is waiting for sons and daughters to walk in their true identity. It is time to break free from the orphan mindset and embrace the Father's love.

Embrace Your Inheritance

The Father's love is freely given—we do not have to earn it, and we do not have to beg for it. We only need to receive it.

"Everything I have is yours." – Luke 15:31 NIV

Activation Prayer

Father, I receive Your love today. I renounce the orphan mindset. I declare that I am fully accepted as Your child. I receive my inheritance as a son/daughter of God. Thank You for welcoming me home. Amen.

Discussion Questions

1. How do you see the orphan mindset at work in the lives of both the younger and older sons in Luke 15? In what ways have you struggled with similar thoughts or attitudes in your own relationship with God?

2. Why is it so significant that the Father restored the younger son immediately—with a robe, a ring, and sandals—rather than making him prove his repentance? What does this teach us about God's grace and our identity?

3. The older brother lived in the Father's house but still felt like a servant. What practical steps can we take to move from striving and entitlement into true sonship and intimacy with the Father?

4

WALKING IN YOUR KINGDOM IDENTITY

Jesus didn't just come to forgive our sins—He came to restore our identity. He didn't just save us from hell; He rescued us from an orphan mindset and brought us back into sonship. Many believers live their lives as servants or slaves, trying to earn God's love and approval. But Jesus showed us what true humanity was meant to look like. He called Himself the Son of Man, not because He was denying His divinity, but because He was revealing our true design—a life lived in perfect relationship with the Father.

"The Son can do nothing by Himself; He only does what He sees His Father doing." – John 5:19 NIV

Jesus didn't operate independently. He didn't live by His own strength. He lived from the Father's voice, presence, and love. And He came to show us how to do the same.

Jesus, the Firstborn of Many Sons

"For those God foreknew He also predestined to be conformed to the

image of His Son, that He might be the firstborn among many brothers and sisters." – Romans 8:29 NIV

Jesus is the firstborn of many sons and daughters. That means He came as our example, not just our Savior. He didn't come just to be worshiped—He came to be imitated.

Jesus Lived as a Son, Not a Servant

Throughout His ministry, Jesus walked in unshakable confidence in His identity. He knew:

- Who He was (Son of God)
- Who His Father was (Abba, loving and present)
- What His mission was (to bring heaven to earth)

He did not live in fear. He did not strive to prove Himself. He walked in rest, authority, and power—and He did it all as a son of the Father. And here's the truth: We are called to live the same way.

"To them that received Him, He gave the right to become children of God." – John 1:12 NASB

Sonship is not something we achieve—it is something we receive.

The Two Identities: Orphans vs. Sons

Many believers mentally understand that they are children of God, but they still live like spiritual orphans. Here's the difference between an orphan mindset and a sonship mindset:

Orphan Spirit	Spirit of Sonship
Works for approval	Works from approval
Lives in fear	Lives in love
Feels distant from God	Feels close to the <u>Father</u>
Strives for blessing	Inherits blessing
Seeks identity in achievements	Finds identity in the <u>Father</u>
Asks, "What must I do?"	Declares, "I am His"

Many Christians live like orphans in the Father's house. They pray like beggars, worship like slaves, and live in fear of losing God's love. But true sons walk in confidence.

"You did not receive a spirit of slavery to fall back into fear, but you received the Spirit of adoption as sons, by whom we cry, 'Abba! Father!'" – Romans 8:15 ESV

Orphans pray for what sons already have. Sons walk in inheritance.

The Power of Knowing Your Identity

Jesus was tempted in the wilderness, but notice how the enemy attacked Him:

"If You are the Son of God, tell these stones to become bread." – Matthew 4:3 NIV

Satan's primary weapon was identity doubt. He wanted Jesus to question who He was. This is the same way the enemy attacks us.

- He tells us we are not truly forgiven.
- He tells us we are not really loved.
- He tells us we are not good enough to be called sons and daughters.

But Jesus never fell for it—because He was secure in the Father's love.

"This is My beloved Son, in whom I am well pleased." –Matthew 3:17 NKJV

Before Jesus ever performed a miracle or preached a sermon, the Father declared His love and pleasure over Him. The same is true for us. We do not earn the Father's love— we receive it.

Sons Have Inheritance

Jesus did not live as a beggar—He lived as an heir. And He came to give us the same inheritance.

"Now if we are children, then we are heirs—heirs of God and co-heirs with Christ." – Romans 8:17 NIV

This means:

- We have access to everything the Father has
- We do not have to work for God's blessings—they are already ours
- We can live in confidence and authority

Imagine a prince who grows up thinking he is a servant. He lives in the palace, but he never dares to sit at the king's table. He works hard every day, hoping that one day he will be noticed. But the truth is, he was always a son. He didn't have to earn his place —he only needed to realize who he was.

"My son, you are always with me, and everything I have is yours." – Luke 15:31 NIV

This is the Father's message to us. Everything He has already belongs to us—we simply need to walk in it.

Living as Sons on Earth

Many believers know they are sons in heaven, but they live like orphans on earth. But true sons and daughters bring the Kingdom to earth.

> *"Your Kingdom come, Your will be done, on earth as it is in heaven." – Matthew 6:10 NKJV*

Sons are called to:

- Walk in supernatural authority (Luke 10:19)
- Release the Father's love (John 13:35)
- Manifest the Kingdom of God (Romans 8:19)

Paul tells us:

> *"The creation waits in eager expectation for the children of God to be revealed." – Romans 8:19 NIV*

The world is not waiting for more religious people—it is waiting for sons and daughters to step into their identity.

How to Walk in Your Identity as a Son or Daughter

Many people mentally believe they are sons and daughters of God, but they struggle to walk in that reality. Here are some practical steps:

1. Renew Your Mind with the Truth

Your mind must be transformed by God's Word. Read, declare, and meditate on who God says you are.

"Be transformed by the renewing of your mind." – Romans 12:2 NKJV

2. Stop Striving – Start Receiving

You do not have to earn God's love. Rest in the truth of your adoption.

"It is finished." – John 19:30 NKJV

3. Spend Time with the Father

Sonship is built on relationship. Spend time in the Father's presence, just as Jesus did.

"Jesus often withdrew to lonely places and prayed." – Luke 5:16 NIV

4. Declare Your Identity Daily

Speak life over yourself. Declare:

- "I am a child of God."
- "I am fully loved and accepted."
- "I carry the Father's authority and inheritance."

You Are a Son, Not a Slave

The Father is saying to you:

"You are always with Me, and everything I have is yours." – Luke 15:31 NIV

You don't have to strive, beg, or prove yourself. You are already a son, already an heir, already loved. Walk in your identity. Live from sonship. Step into your inheritance.

Activation Prayer

Father, I receive my identity as Your child. I renounce the orphan mindset. I choose to live as a son, not a servant. I receive my inheritance in Christ. Thank You for calling me Your own. Amen.

Discussion Questions

1. Why is it significant that Jesus called Himself the "Son of Man"? How does this title help us understand our own identity and design as children of God?

2. What are some specific ways the orphan mindset still shows up in the lives of believers—even those who know they are saved? How can we shift from striving to receiving?

3. Romans 8:19 says creation is waiting for the children of God to be revealed. What does it look like in your life to walk in your identity as a son or daughter—and how might that impact the world around you?

5

ABBA'S INHERITANCE
WHAT SONS RECIEVE

A true father always leaves an inheritance for his children. In the Kingdom, this is no different. God is not just a Master, and we are not just servants—He is a Father, and we are His sons and daughters. Many believers live like spiritual beggars, constantly asking God for things they already have access to.

But the truth is, as sons and daughters of God, we have been given full access to the inheritance of the Kingdom. We are not meant to live in lack, fear, or uncertainty—we are meant to live in abundance, authority, and security. Paul reminds us:

"Now if we are children, then we are heirs—heirs of God and co-heirs with Christ." – Romans 8:17 NIV

Jesus didn't just come to forgive our sins—He came to restore our inheritance. He came to bring us back into the family, giving us everything that belongs to Him. This chapter will explore what that inheritance looks like and how to walk in it daily.

You Are an Heir of the Kingdom

When we hear the word inheritance, we often think of material wealth—something passed down after someone dies. But in the Kingdom, inheritance is not just about things—it is about identity, authority, and access. Paul says:

"You did not receive a spirit of slavery to fall back into fear, but you received the Spirit of adoption as sons, by whom we cry out, 'Abba! Father!'" – Romans 8:15 ESV

This means that, through Christ, we have been legally adopted into God's family. And as children, we have the same rights and privileges as Jesus Himself.

"The Father has qualified you to share in the inheritance of His holy people in the Kingdom of light." – Colossians 1:12 NIV

What Is the Inheritance of Sons?

Sons do not work for an inheritance—they receive it by birthright. As children of God, we have been given an inheritance in Christ that includes:

1. The Father's Presence – Full Access to God

- In the Old Testament, people had to go through priests to approach God.
- But through Jesus, the veil was torn (Matthew 27:51), and now we have direct access to the Father.
- "Let us then approach God's throne of grace with confidence." – Hebrews 4:16

2. The Holy Spirit – The Spirit of Sonship

- The Holy Spirit is the seal of our adoption and inheritance (Ephesians 1:13-14).

- He is the proof that we belong to the Father and the guarantee of our sonship.
- "Because you are sons, God sent the Spirit of His Son into our hearts, crying, 'Abba, Father!'" – Galatians 4:6

3. Authority Over the Enemy – Sons Walk in Dominion

- Jesus gave us authority over all the power of the enemy (Luke 10:19).
- Orphans live in fear, but sons walk in confidence and victory.
- "You will tread upon the lion and the cobra; you will trample the great lion and the serpent." – Psalm 91:13

4. The Father's Provision – No More Lack

- Orphans worry about survival, but sons trust in their Father's provision.
- "Do not worry... your heavenly Father knows what you need." – Matthew 6:31-32
- God's Kingdom operates in abundance, not scarcity.

5. The Power of the Kingdom – Sons Carry Heaven on Earth

- Jesus said we have been given the keys to the Kingdom (Matthew 16:19).
- Sons have the authority to release heaven's power on earth.
- "Your Kingdom come, Your will be done, on earth as it is in heaven." – Matthew 6:10

Sons vs. Servants: How Do You See Yourself?

Many believers are living like servants, constantly begging God for things they already have access to. The difference between a servant mindset and a sonship mindset is crucial:

Servants	Sons
Work for acceptance	Live from acceptance
Beg for blessings	Receive inheritance
See God as a master	See God as a Father
Live in fear	Live in confidence
Ask, "What must I do?"	Declare, "I am His"

The Story of the Older Brother – Inheritance Without Relationship

In Luke 15:25-31, the older brother in the parable of the Prodigal Son lived in the Father's house but never accessed his inheritance. When he saw his younger brother restored, he became angry and said:

"All these years I've been slaving for you and never disobeyed your orders, yet you never gave me even a young goat so I could celebrate with my friends." – Luke 15:29 NIV

This is the orphan mindset in action. The older son was in the house but didn't know what belonged to him. The Father's response is key:

"My son, you are always with me, and everything I have is yours." – Luke 15:31 NIV

Many believers live in the Father's house (salvation) but never experience the fullness of their inheritance. They are still working to earn something that already belongs to them.

How to Walk in Your Inheritance

1. Believe You Are a Son

- The first step to walking in inheritance is accepting your sonship.
- "To those who believed in His name, He gave the right to become children of God." – John 1:12

2. Stop Striving – Start Receiving

- You don't have to work for what has already been given to you.
- Rest in the fact that the Father's love and inheritance are freely yours.

3. Declare Your Sonship Daily
Speak these declarations over yourself:

- "I am a child of God and an heir of the Kingdom."
- "Everything the Father has is mine."
- "I do not lack—I have access to abundance."

4. Walk in Kingdom Authority

- Sons don't ask for authority—they walk in it.
- When you understand your identity, you can speak to mountains, heal the sick, and cast out fear.

"For the earnest expectation of the creation eagerly waits for the revealing of the sons of God." – Romans 8:19 NKJV

The world is not waiting for more religious people—it is waiting for sons and daughters to walk in their inheritance.

Everything the Father Has is Yours

You are not a beggar in the Kingdom. You are not an outsider. You are not a slave. You are a son. Everything the Father has is already yours. It's time to step into your inheritance and walk in your full identity.

"Fear not, little flock, for it is your Father's good pleasure to give you the Kingdom." – Luke 12:32 NKJV

Activation Prayer

Father, I receive my inheritance in Christ. I renounce every orphan mindset that keeps me from walking in sonship. I declare that I am Your child, and I have full access to the Kingdom. I choose to walk in my inheritance, authority, and abundance. Everything You have is mine, and I will live as a son/daughter of the King. Amen.

Discussion Questions

1. What are some areas in your life where you may still be living like a spiritual beggar or servant—asking God for what He's already given you in Christ? How can you shift to receiving and walking in your inheritance as a son or daughter?

2. The older brother lived in the Father's house but never accessed his inheritance. Why do you think many believers struggle to enjoy the benefits of sonship, even after salvation?

3. Which part of your Kingdom inheritance—presence, provision, authority, identity, or power—do you most need to grow in right now? What steps can you take to walk more fully in it this week?

6

THE POWER OF SONSHIP IN DAILY LIFE

W alking in sonship is not just a theological concept—it is meant to transform every aspect of our lives. True sonship affects how we see ourselves, how we relate to others, and how we engage with the world around us.

Many believers know they are children of God in their minds, but they still live like spiritual orphans in their daily lives. They struggle with fear, striving, insecurity, and identity confusion. But once we begin to walk in the reality of sonship, everything changes.

Jesus modeled sonship perfectly. He was never anxious, never insecure, and never afraid—because He lived from the certainty of His Father's love and authority. In this chapter, we will explore how true sonship impacts:

1. Your relationship with God – Moving from religious duty to intimacy
2. Your personal identity – Living in confidence and security

3. Your relationships – Loving others from a place of wholeness
4. Your leadership – Leading with love, not fear
5. Your faith and prayer life – Operating in supernatural authority

Sons Walk in Confidence, Not Fear

One of the greatest differences between an orphan and a son is how they respond to fear and uncertainty.

Orphan Mindset	Sonship Mindset
Lives in fear of rejection	Lives in confidence of love
Always striving for approval	Rests in the Father's acceptance
Feels unworthy of God's blessings	Receives blessings freely
Afraid of failure	Secure in identity
Asks, "What if I am not enough?"	Declares, "I am already chosen"

Fear is the language of an orphan, but confidence is the language of a son.

"For you did not receive a spirit of slavery to fall back into fear, but you received the Spirit of adoption as sons, by whom we cry, 'Abba! Father!'" – Romans 8:15 ESV

Sons do not fear lack, rejection, or failure—because they know they are fully loved, fully accepted, and fully provided for.

Sons Walk in Intimacy, Not Performance

Many Christians still live in a servant mindset, trying to earn God's love through religious performance. They believe that if they pray enough, read enough, and serve enough, then God will be pleased with them. But sons don't serve to be accepted—they serve because they are already accepted.

"The Son can do nothing by Himself; He only does what He sees His Father doing." – John 5:19 NIV

Jesus never performed for the Father—He simply walked in relationship. He knew the Father's heart, and everything He did flowed from that intimacy.

Practical Steps to Deepen Intimacy with the Father:

1. Prioritize relationship over routine – Spend time with God as a Father, not just a duty.
2. Learn to listen – Sons don't just talk; they listen to the Father's voice (John 10:27).
3. Stop striving, start receiving – God's love is not earned; it is freely given.
4. Live from rest – Sons don't worry about tomorrow because they trust the Father (Matthew 6:25-26).

"You are always with me, and everything I have is yours." – Luke 15:31 NIV

Sons Love from Wholeness, Not Neediness

When you know you are loved by the Father, you don't need to seek validation from people. You are free to love others selflessly. Many relationships are broken because people are trying to get something from others that only the Father can give. But true sons and daughters walk in wholeness.

"We love because He first loved us." – 1 John 4:19 ESV

How Sonship Transforms Relationships:

- In Marriage – You stop expecting your spouse to fill a void only God can fill.

- In Friendships – You don't need to be approved by people because you are already approved by God.
- In Family – You reflect the Father's heart to your children, parents, and siblings.
- In Community – You bring love and healing to broken relationships.

Sons love freely because they have freely received love.

Sons Lead with Love, Not Control

The world's leadership is based on power, control, and position. But Kingdom leadership is based on love, servanthood, and identity.

"Whoever wants to be great among you must be your servant." –
Matthew 20:26 NIV

Leaders with an orphan mindset lead from insecurity, control, and fear. They dominate others to feel important. But sons lead from love, humility, and confidence.

Orphan Leadership	Sonship Leadership
Leads from insecurity	Leads from identity
Controls people	Empowers people
Demands respect	Earns Respect
Seeks power	Serves with love

If you are called to lead (whether in ministry, business, or family), your greatest leadership asset is knowing you are a son or daughter first.

Sons Walk in Supernatural Authority

Sons carry the Father's authority because they are heirs of the Kingdom.

"I have given you authority to trample on snakes and scorpions and to overcome all the power of the enemy." –Luke 10:19 NIV

Orphans vs. Sons in Prayer:

- Orphans beg God for power – Sons use the authority they already have.
- Orphans pray timid prayers – Sons pray bold, faith-filled prayers.
- Orphans ask for permission – Sons declare Kingdom realities.

Jesus never begged the Father for miracles—He commanded healing, peace, and breakthrough. And He gave us that same authority.

"Truly, truly, I say to you, whoever believes in Me will do the works that I do, and greater works than these will he do." – John 14:12 ESV

It's time to stop asking for things that God already gave us and start walking in them.

How to Walk in Sonship Daily

1. Start Your Day in the Father's Love

- Begin each morning by reminding yourself of your identity.
- Declare: "I am a son/daughter of the King."

2. Replace Fear with Confidence

- Whenever fear rises, speak God's promises over yourself (Romans 8:15).

- Fear has no place in a son's life!

3. Serve from Identity, Not Obligation

- Whether at work, church, or home, serve from love, not pressure.

4. Walk in Boldness and Authority

- Pray with confidence, knowing you are an heir to the Kingdom.
- Speak life over your situations, family, and future.

5. Stay Connected to the Father's Presence

- Spend daily time with Abba Father—not out of obligation, but out of relationship.
- *"Draw near to God, and He will draw near to you."* – James 4:8

Sonship Changes Everything

You were not made to live in fear, striving, or insecurity. You were made to live as a beloved son or daughter—secure, loved, and empowered. Everything Jesus walked in belongs to you. The Father is inviting you to step into your true identity today.

"Fear not, little flock, for it is your Father's good pleasure to give you the Kingdom." – Luke 12:32 NKJV

Activation Prayer

Father, I receive my identity as Your son/daughter. I renounce fear, striving, and insecurity. I choose to walk in confidence, authority, and love. I declare that I am fully accepted, fully empowered, and fully Yours. Let me live every day from my inheritance in You.
Amen.

Discussion Questions

1 . Which area of your life—identity, relationships, leadership, or prayer—do you find most affected by an orphan mindset? What would it look like to live from sonship in that area instead?

2 . Jesus never operated from fear or striving. How can you practically cultivate intimacy with the Father so that your daily life flows from rest, love, and confidence rather than performance or anxiety?

3 . The chapter says, "Sons carry the Father's authority." What would change in your prayer life, decisions, or leadership if you truly believed you had Kingdom authority as a son or daughter of God?

7

SONS WALK IN LOVE NOT FEAR

Fear is one of the greatest barriers to sonship. It is the language of orphans and the greatest tool of the enemy to keep believers from walking in their true identity. When Adam and Eve sinned, their first reaction was fear—they hid from the Father because they believed they had lost His love.

But sons and daughters of God are not meant to live in fear. The Father's love is perfect, unshakable, and eternal. When we truly experience His love, fear loses its power over us.

"There is no fear in love. But perfect love drives out fear." – 1 John 4:18 NIV

In this chapter, we will explore how fear is broken through sonship, how love transforms our relationship with God and others, and how to walk in boldness, confidence, and security.

Fear is the Language of Orphans

The orphan spirit thrives on fear—fear of rejection, fear of lack, fear of failure. An orphan constantly feels like they must fight for approval because they don't believe they are truly loved. When Adam and Eve sinned, they hid from God:

"I heard You in the garden, and I was afraid because I was naked; so I hid." – Genesis 3:10 NIV

Fear always leads to hiding—from God, from people, from our calling. But sons don't hide—they run to the Father. Jesus never lived in fear. He walked in perfect love and confidence because He knew who He was. He invites us to do the same.

"For you did not receive a spirit of slavery leading to fear again, but you received the Spirit of adoption as sons, by whom we cry, 'Abba! Father!'" – Romans 8:15 NASB

Sons live in love and security—they don't run from the Father; they run to Him.

Love is the Foundation of Sonship

Many believers struggle with fear, insecurity, and striving because they have never truly encountered the Father's love.

"See what great love the Father has lavished on us, that we should be called children of God! And that is what we are!" – 1 John 3:1 NIV

The foundation of sonship is love. If we don't believe we are fully loved, we will always live in fear and performance.

How the Father's Love Transforms Us

1. Love replaces striving – Sons don't work for love; they rest in it.
2. Love casts out fear – We don't fear failure or rejection when we are secure.

3. Love empowers boldness – When we are loved, we live with confidence.
4. Love overflows to others – We love others as we have been loved.

"We love because He first loved us." – 1 John 4:19 ESV

Fear vs. Love: The Two Mindsets

Orphan Spirit (Fear-Based)	Spirit of Sonship (Love-Based)
Tries to earn love	Knows they are already loved
Fears rejection	Walks in acceptance
Lives in anxiety	Lives in peace
Serves out of duty	Serves out of love
Hides from God	Runs to God

Fear cripples people, but love empowers people. When we fully embrace our identity as sons, fear no longer controls us.

Sons Walk in Boldness and Authority

Because Jesus lived in perfect love, He walked in boldness and authority.

"The wicked flee when no one pursues, but the righteous are bold as a lion." – Proverbs 28:1 ESV

Sons carry confidence because they know their Father is with them.

What Boldness Looks Like in Everyday Life

1. Boldness in Prayer – Sons pray with authority, not begging like orphans (Luke 10:19).
2. Boldness in Relationships – Sons love without fear of rejection (1 John 4:19).

3. Boldness in Calling – Sons step out in faith, knowing the Father backs them (Romans 8:31).
4. Boldness in Spiritual Warfare – Sons do not fear the enemy; they walk in victory (Luke 10:19).

"God has not given us a spirit of fear, but of power, love, and a sound mind." – 2 Timothy 1:7 NKJV

If you struggle with fear, doubt, or insecurity, it's not because you are weak—it's because the enemy wants you to forget who you are. It's time to reject fear and walk in the boldness of sonship.

How to Overcome Fear and Walk in Love

Fear is not broken by willpower—it is broken by experiencing the Father's love.

1. Receive the Father's Love Daily

- Spend time in prayer, worship, and scripture focused on God's love.
- Meditate on key sonship scriptures (Romans 8:15, 1 John 4:18).
- Ask the Holy Spirit to reveal the Father's love in a deeper way.

2. Replace Lies with Truth

Fear thrives on lies. Identify the lies you believe and replace them with truth.

- Lie: "I am not enough."
- Truth: "I am fully accepted in Christ" (Ephesians 1:6).

- Lie: "God is disappointed in me."
- Truth: "I am His beloved child" (1 John 3:1).
- Lie: "I have to prove my worth."
- Truth: "I am already chosen and loved" (John 15:16).

3. Declare Your Identity Daily

Speak life and identity over yourself every day. Say out loud:

- "I am a child of God, and I am loved."
- "I have no fear because perfect love casts out fear."
- "I walk in boldness, confidence, and authority."

"Death and life are in the power of the tongue." – Proverbs 18:21 NKJV

4. Step Out in Faith

- Fear is broken when we do the very thing we are afraid of.
- Take bold steps—pray for people, share your faith, walk in confidence.

"Be strong and courageous. Do not be afraid, for the Lord your God is with you wherever you go." – Joshua 1:9 NIV

Sons do not shrink back. They walk in faith and courage.

Walk in Love, Not Fear

Fear is not your portion. You were created to walk in love, security, and confidence. Jesus never lived in fear, and as His brothers and sisters, we are called to live the same way. The Father is saying:

"Fear not, for I am with you. I have called you by name, and you are Mine." – Isaiah 43:1 NKJV

You are fully loved. Fully accepted. Fully free. Walk in love, not fear.

Activation Prayer

Father, I renounce fear, insecurity, and striving. I receive Your perfect love that casts out all fear. I declare that I am Your child, fully accepted, fully loved. I walk in boldness, confidence, and faith. Thank You for setting me free from fear. I choose to live as a son/daughter, not an orphan. Amen.

Discussion Questions

1. Why do you think fear is so closely tied to the orphan spirit? How has fear shown up in your relationship with God, others, or your calling—and how does sonship offer a different way to live?

2. The chapter says, "Fear is not broken by willpower—it is broken by experiencing the Father's love." What does it practically look like in your life to receive the Father's love daily?

3. What bold step can you take this week to walk in your identity as a son or daughter of God—whether in prayer, relationships, leadership, or spiritual warfare?

8

INTIMACY WITH THE FATHER
THE KEY TO EVERYTHING

Sonship is not just about identity—it is about relationship. True sons and daughters walk closely with the Father, not as servants fulfilling religious duties, but as beloved children who enjoy intimacy with Him. Many believers struggle with feeling distant from God. They know they are saved, but they do not experience the deep friendship that Jesus had with the Father. But here is the truth:

"You are always with Me, and everything I have is yours." – Luke 15:31 NIV

God is not far away. He is always near, always present, and always inviting us into deeper intimacy. In this chapter, we will explore how intimacy with the Father:

1. Transforms our relationship with God
2. Replaces religion with love
3. Gives us access to the Father's voice and presence
4. Empowers us to walk in supernatural sonship

Jesus Modeled Intimacy with the Father

Jesus did not just come to die for our sins—He came to show us what life as a son looks like. He walked in constant intimacy with the Father.

"The Father who dwells in Me does His works." – John 14:10 NKJV

Jesus did not act independently—everything He did flowed from His relationship with the Father.

"The Son can do nothing by Himself; He only does what He sees His Father doing." – John 5:19 NIV

This was the secret to His life and ministry: He lived from closeness, not distance. If Jesus, the perfect Son of God, needed intimacy with the Father, how much more do we?

Religion vs. Relationship – The Difference in Mindset

Many Christians today live in religion, not relationship. They see God as a Master to serve, rather than a Father to know.

Religious Mindset	Sonship Mindset
Tries to earn God's love	Receives God's love freely
Feels distant from God	Walks in intimacy with God
Serves from obligation	Serves from love
Sees God as a Master	Sees God as a Father
Fears failure	Trusts in love

A religious spirit says:

- "If I pray enough, God will love me more."
- "If I read the Bible every day, I will be more accepted."
- "If I serve, God will be pleased with me."

But sons do not work for love—they work from love.

"We love because He first loved us." – 1 John 4:19 ESV

Jesus' High Priestly Prayer – Our Oneness with the Father

On the night before His crucifixion, Jesus prayed what is known as His High Priestly Prayer in John 17. In this prayer, Jesus revealed the greatest desire of His heart—that we, as sons and daughters, would experience the same oneness with the Father that He had.

"I have given them the glory that You gave Me, that they may be one as We are one—I in them and You in Me—so that they may be brought to complete unity. Then the world will know that You sent Me and have loved them even as You have loved Me." – John 17:22-23 NIV

This passage is mind-blowing. Jesus is saying:

1. The same relationship that He had with the Father is now available to us.

- Jesus lived in perfect oneness with the Father, and He invites us into that same intimacy.
- This means we are not just followers of Christ—we are fully included in the divine family.

2. The Father loves us as much as He loves Jesus.

- Read that again: "Then the world will know that You... have loved them even as You have loved Me."
- This is not a lesser love—it is the exact same love that the Father has for Jesus!
- Many believers struggle to accept this truth, but Jesus Himself declared it.

3. What This Means for Us

- You are fully accepted in the Father's love.
- You are as close to the Father as Jesus is.
- You do not have to strive for approval—you already have it.

This is why Jesus came—to bring us back into the same relationship with the Father that He enjoyed.

Direct Access to the Father – Jesus' Teaching in John 16

Before Jesus went to the cross, He told His disciples something revolutionary:

"In that day you will ask in My name. I am not saying that I will ask the Father on your behalf. No, the Father Himself loves you because you have loved Me and have believed that I came from God." – John 16:26-27 NIV

This is a radical shift in how we relate to God.

1. We no longer need an intermediary to talk to the Father.

- Before Jesus, people had to go through priests, prophets, or sacrifices to approach God.
- But now, as sons and daughters, we have direct access to the Father.

2. Jesus makes it clear: "You are not praying to Me—you are praying to the Father."

- This does not mean we dishonor Jesus—it means we step fully into our sonship.

- Jesus was saying, "You are not just My followers—you are My brothers and sisters in the family of God."

3. The Father Himself loves you.

- Jesus emphasizes this: "The Father Himself loves you."
- He is telling us, "You don't need to convince the Father to love you—He already does."

The Power of Praying as Sons

Many believers pray like orphans—begging, pleading, and hoping God will answer. But Jesus says, "No, you are sons and daughters. Go directly to the Father."

"Let us then approach God's throne of grace with confidence, so that we may receive mercy and find grace to help us in our time of need."
– Hebrews 4:16 NIV

Sons do not beg—they ask boldly because they know they are loved.

The Father is Calling You Closer

The greatest treasure of sonship is knowing the Father personally. His love is always available, and He is inviting you into deeper intimacy. If you've ever felt distant from God, the Father is saying:

"You are always with Me, and everything I have is yours." *– Luke 15:31 NIV*

Come close. Sit at His feet. Listen to His voice. Rest in His love. He is not just your God—He is your Father.

Activation Prayer

Father, I choose intimacy with You over religion. I renounce every mindset that keeps me distant from Your love. I receive my identity as Your beloved child. I declare that I hear Your voice and walk in Your presence daily. Let me live every moment in deep communion with You. Amen.

Discussion Questions

1. Many believers know they are saved but still feel distant from God. What do you think keeps people from experiencing deep intimacy with the Father—and how can that begin to change?

2. Jesus said the Father loves us as much as He loves Him (John 17:23). How does that truth challenge or encourage you? What would change if you really believed it in your heart, not just your head?

3. What does it practically look like to prioritize relationship with the Father over religious performance in your daily life —especially in how you pray, read Scripture, or serve?

9

SONS OPERATE IN SUPERNATURAL POWER

Sonship is not just about identity and relationship—it is about authority and power. When we step into our true identity as sons and daughters of God, we are given the same authority that Jesus walked in. Many believers live powerless lives because they do not realize that supernatural power is their inheritance. They pray timid prayers, struggle with fear, and hope that God will do something—without realizing that He has already given them the authority to act. But Jesus made it clear:

"Truly, truly, I say to you, whoever believes in Me will do the works that I do, and greater works than these will he do, because I am going to the Father." – John 14:12 ESV

If Jesus is the firstborn among many brothers and sisters (Romans 8:29), then that means we are called to walk just as He did—in boldness, authority, and power. This chapter will explore how sons and daughters of God operate in supernatural power, how to break free from a powerless mindset, and how to walk in miracles, healing, and Kingdom authority.

Jesus – The Model of Sonship and Power

Jesus did not just come to die for our sins—He came to show us what it looks like to walk in sonship. Everything He did— healing the sick, casting out demons, calming storms, multiplying food, raising the dead—He did as a man filled with the Holy Spirit, demonstrating how we are supposed to live.

"The Spirit of the Lord is upon Me, because He has anointed Me to proclaim good news to the poor. He has sent Me to proclaim liberty to the captives and recovery of sight to the blind, to set at liberty those who are oppressed." – Luke 4:18 ESV

Jesus was anointed by the Holy Spirit, and now, through Him, we are anointed as well:

"As the Father has sent Me, so I am sending you." – John 20:21 NLT

This means that everything Jesus did, we are called to do. He did not walk in supernatural power just because He was God— He did it because He was a Son operating under the Father's authority.

Sons Walk in Authority, Not Fear

Orphans live in fear and uncertainty, but sons walk in confidence and authority.

"For God has not given us a spirit of fear, but of power, love, and a sound mind." – 2 Timothy 1:7 NKJV

Many believers beg God for power, but Jesus never told us to beg—He told us to use the authority we already have.

"I have given you authority to tread on serpents and scorpions, and

over all the power of the enemy, and nothing shall hurt you." – Luke
10:19 ESV

Jesus has already given us authority over:

1. Sickness – We have power to heal the sick (Mark
    16:18).
2. The demonic – We have power to cast out demons
    (Mark 16:17).
3. Lack and need – We have power to release provision
    (Philippians 4:19).
4. Fear and doubt – We have power to walk in boldness
    (2 Timothy 1:7).

Sons do not ask for permission to use what has already been
given to them—they walk in it boldly.

"The righteous are bold as a lion." – Proverbs 28:1 ESV

The Holy Spirit – The Power Source of Sons

The key to supernatural power is not trying harder—it is
being filled with the Holy Spirit.

"But you shall receive power when the Holy Spirit has come upon
you; and you shall be witnesses to Me" – Acts 1:8 NKJV

Jesus did not perform any miracles until He was baptized in
the Holy Spirit (Luke 3:22, Luke 4:1). If Jesus needed the Holy
Spirit's power, how much more do we? What Happens When
Sons Are Filled with the Holy Spirit?

1. They walk in boldness – Peter went from denying
    Jesus to preaching with fire (Acts 2:14).

2. They speak with power – Paul's words were not just talk, but demonstrations of power (1 Corinthians 2:4).

3. They heal the sick – Everywhere the apostles went, people were healed (Acts 5:15-16).

4. They shift atmospheres – Sons carry heaven's reality everywhere they go.

If you want to walk in supernatural power, the key is to be filled daily with the Holy Spirit.

"Be continually filled with the Spirit." – Ephesians 5:18 AMP

Sons Do What Their Father Does

Jesus lived in perfect obedience to the Father:

"The Son can do nothing by Himself; He only does what He sees the Father doing." – John 5:19 NIV

This means that when Jesus healed, He was revealing the Father's heart to heal. When Jesus cast out demons, He was revealing the Father's heart to set people free. When we walk as sons, we are not just doing ministry—we are revealing the Father's heart to the world.

"As He is, so are we in this world." – 1 John 4:17 NKJV

How to Walk in Supernatural Power as a Son

Many people think power is for a select few, but the truth is supernatural power is the inheritance of every son and daughter of God.

1. Believe That Supernatural Power Is Your Inheritance

- Many Christians are waiting for power, but Jesus already gave it.
- Stop waiting—step into it by faith (Mark 16:17-18).

2. Be Filled with the Holy Spirit Daily

- The baptism of the Holy Spirit is essential for supernatural power (Acts 1:8).
- Pray: "Father, fill me with Your Spirit and power."

3. Pray Bold, Commanding Prayers

- Jesus never prayed, "God, please heal this person."
- He commanded healing: "Be healed."
- Sons pray with authority, not doubt.

4. Take Risks and Step Out in Faith

- Pray for people in public, at work, at home—everywhere.
- Sons are not afraid of failure—they step out boldly.

5. Expect Miracles to Happen

- Sons do not beg for miracles—they expect them.
- Walk in the confidence of your inheritance (Romans 8:17).

"Heal the sick, raise the dead, cleanse lepers, cast out demons. Freely you have received; freely give." – Matthew 10:8 NKJV

You Were Made for Supernatural Living

The world does not need more powerless Christians—it needs

sons and daughters walking in Kingdom authority. Jesus is inviting you to step into your full inheritance:

- To heal the sick
- To cast out demons
- To shift atmospheres
- To release heaven on earth

You were not made for fear and timidity—you were made to walk in power and authority. The Father is saying:

"Everything I have is yours." – Luke 15:31 NIV

It's time to step into your inheritance and release heaven on earth.

Activation Prayer

Father, I receive my inheritance as Your son/daughter. I renounce fear, doubt, and a powerless mindset. I declare that I am filled with the Holy Spirit and power. I will walk in miracles, signs, and wonders as Jesus did. I release heaven on earth through my life. Amen.

Discussion Questions

1. Why do you think so many believers live powerless lives even though Jesus promised we would do the same works He did—and greater (John 14:12)? What mindsets or beliefs need to shift?

2. Jesus operated in power as a man filled with the Holy Spirit. What does this reveal about our potential as sons and daughters of God today? How can you grow in being filled and led by the Spirit daily?

3. Which area of supernatural authority—healing, spiritual warfare, boldness, miracles—do you feel most called to grow in? What step can you take this week to walk in that authority by faith?

10

SONS BRING KINGDOM CULTURE TO THE EARTH

Sonship is not just about identity and intimacy—it is about responsibility. When we step into sonship, we are not only receiving from the Father; we are also called to build His Kingdom on earth. The Hebrew word for son is "Ben" (בֵּן), which means "the builder of the Father's house." This reveals a powerful truth: Sons are not just loved; they are entrusted. Many believers think sonship is just about receiving love from the Father, but true sons carry the Father's heart and His mission.

"For to us a child is born, to us a son is given, and the government will be on His shoulders." – Isaiah 9:6 NIV

Jesus did not come just as a child—He came as a Son, carrying the government of God. And now, as co-heirs with Christ, we are called to carry that same Kingdom government on the earth.

This chapter will explore how sons:

1. Advance the Father's Kingdom
2. Carry His government and authority
3. Transform culture through sonship

4. Build the Father's house on the earth

Sons Carry the Father's Government

Isaiah 9:6 says: "A child is born, a son is given, and the government will rest on His shoulders." NLT

This verse reveals a critical truth: Children are loved, but sons are entrusted with government. Jesus, as the firstborn Son, was given Kingdom authority to rule and reign. And now, as sons and daughters of God, we have been given the same governmental authority in the Spirit. Paul confirms this:

"If we are children, then we are heirs—heirs of God and co-heirs with Christ." – Romans 8:17 NIV

What Does It Mean to Carry the Government of God?

- Sons are ambassadors of heaven (2 Corinthians 5:20).
- Sons bring heaven's solutions to earth (Matthew 6:10).
- Sons exercise authority over darkness (Luke 10:19).
- Sons release justice and righteousness (Isaiah 9:7).

Many believers live as powerless spectators, waiting for God to act. But sons are given the authority to act on behalf of their Father. Jesus said:

"I will give you the keys of the Kingdom of heaven; whatever you bind on earth will be bound in heaven, and whatever you loose on earth will be loosed in heaven." –Matthew 16:19 NIV

Sons do not wait for heaven to move—they release heaven on earth.

Sons Build the Father's House

The word "Ben" (בֵּן) in Hebrew means "the builder of the Father's house." This means that true sonship is about more than just receiving love—it's about building what the Father desires. Jesus Himself said:

> *"I will build My Church, and the gates of hell shall not prevail against it." – Matthew 16:18 NKJV*

Jesus, as the Son of God, was the ultimate builder of the Father's house. Now, as sons and daughters, we are called to continue that work.

What Does It Mean to Build the Father's House?

1. Expanding the Kingdom of God – Preaching the Gospel, discipling nations (Matthew 28:19).
2. Transforming Culture – Bringing Kingdom values into society.
3. Releasing Heaven on Earth – Walking in supernatural power and authority.
4. Restoring Families and Communities – Bringing the Father's love to broken places.

We are not just called to believe in the Father's Kingdom— we are called to build it.

> *"For the creation waits in eager expectation for the children of God to be revealed." – Romans 8:19 NIV*

The world is waiting for sons and daughters to rise up and establish Kingdom culture on the earth.

Sons Transform Culture Through the Kingdom

The Kingdom of God is not just about personal salvation—it is about cultural transformation. Jesus taught us to pray:

"Your Kingdom come, Your will be done, on earth as it is in heaven." – Matthew 6:10 NKJV

This means that sons and daughters of God are called to bring the culture of heaven into every area of life.

How Sons Influence Culture

Sphere of Influence	How Sons Bring Kingdom Culture
Family	Fathers and mothers raising Kingdom-minded children
Education	Teaching Kingdom values in schools
Government	Bringing righteousness and justice into leadership
Business	Creating wealth with integrity and generosity
Media & Arts	Using creativity to glorify God and inspire truth
Church	Equipping the Body of Christ for supernatural living

Sons do not just participate in culture—they transform it.

"You are the light of the world. A city on a hill cannot be hidden." – Matthew 5:14 ESV

The Father's sons and daughters are called to bring light, love, and transformation into every sphere of society.

Sons Are Entrusted With Inheritance

Many believers live with a poverty mindset, thinking they must beg God for resources and provision. But sons know that inheritance is already theirs.

"Fear not, little flock, for it is your Father's good pleasure to give you the Kingdom." – Luke 12:32 NKJV

Everything that belongs to the Father belongs to His sons. What Does Kingdom Inheritance Look Like?

1. Spiritual Authority – Sons walk in supernatural power (Luke 10:19).
2. Divine Provision – Sons never lack, because the Father is their source (Philippians 4:19).
3. Kingdom Influence – Sons are placed in positions of leadership to shape nations (Daniel 2:21).
4. Eternal Rewards – Sons receive the fullness of their inheritance in eternity (Revelation 3:21).

The Father is looking for sons who are ready to be entrusted with His Kingdom.

"To him who overcomes, I will give the right to sit with Me on My throne." – Revelation 3:21 NKJV

How to Walk as a Son Who Builds the Father's House

Walking as a true son or daughter means stepping into your inheritance and responsibility.

1. Shift from Consumer to Builder

- Sons don't just attend church—they build the Kingdom.
- Ask: "How can I bring heaven to earth?"

2. Live with Kingdom Purpose

- You are not just here to survive—you are here to transform the world.
- Declare: "I am a builder of my Father's house."

3. Take Your Authority Seriously

- Stop waiting for God to move—He is waiting for you to step into your authority.
- Speak, decree, and establish Kingdom reality wherever you go.

4. Influence Your Sphere of Impact

- Wherever you work, study, or serve, bring Kingdom values.
- You are not just an employee, teacher, or artist—you are a son or daughter with a mission.

"The earth is waiting for the sons of God to be revealed." – Romans 8:19 NKJV

The world is waiting for you.

Sons Build Their Father's Kingdom

Sons do not live for themselves—they live for the Father's house.

"Everything I have is yours." – Luke 15:31 NIV

The Father is looking for sons and daughters who will carry His Kingdom, transform culture, and build His house on earth. The question is: Will you answer the call?

Activation Prayer

*Father, I receive my calling as a builder of Your house. I renounce
every orphan mindset that keeps me from stepping into my
inheritance. I declare that I am entrusted with Kingdom authority.
I will bring heaven to earth and build what You desire. Let me be a
light in the world and a carrier of Your Kingdom. Amen.*

Discussion Questions

1 . The Hebrew word for "son" (Ben) means "builder of the
Father's house." How does this redefine your understanding
of what it means to be a son or daughter of God? What might
God be calling you to build?

2 . In what areas of your life—family, work, church, or
community—do you sense God inviting you to shift from
being a consumer to a Kingdom builder? How can you begin to
step into that role this week?

3 . The chapter outlines ways sons are called to influence
culture. Which sphere—family, education, business, government, media, or the church—do you feel most drawn to, and
what would it look like to bring Kingdom culture there?

11

SONS BUILD KINGDOM FAMILY, NOT RELIGION

One of the greatest misunderstandings about the Kingdom of God is that it is about rules, rituals, and religious systems. But Jesus did not come to start a new religion—He came to restore a family.

"I will be a Father to you, and you will be My sons and daughters, says the Lord Almighty." – 2 Corinthians 6:18 NIV

The Church is not a building—it is the Father's family on earth. Sons and daughters are not just called to attend services; they are called to build a Kingdom family that reflects the Father's heart. This chapter will explore:

1. The difference between religion and Kingdom family
2. Why sons and daughters create a culture of love and honor
3. How spiritual fathers and mothers raise up the next generation
4. How the Church is meant to be a family, not an institution

The Difference Between Religion and Kingdom Family

Many people see Christianity as a set of religious rules rather than a relationship with the Father. But Jesus came to break down the barriers of religion and bring us back into family.

Religious Mindset	Kingdom Family Mindset
Focuses on rules and regulations	Focuses on relationship with the Father
Sees God as a Master	Sees God as a Father
Values performance and duty	Values love and intimacy
Divides people into insiders and outsiders	Welcomes all into the father's house
Fears punishment	Walks in love and confidence

Jesus rebuked the Pharisees because they made faith about laws instead of love. He reminded them:

"I desire mercy, not sacrifice." – Matthew 9:13 NIV

Sons do not live under religious pressure—they live in the freedom of family.

Sons and Daughters Create a Culture of Love and Honor

A true Kingdom family is marked by love and honor, not control and fear.

"By this everyone will know that you are My disciples, if you love one another." – John 13:35 NIV

What Does a Kingdom Family Look Like?

1. Unconditional Love – Just like the Father's love, the family of God should be a place where everyone belongs.
2. Honor and Respect – Sons and daughters celebrate

each other's value, rather than competing for position.

3. Healing and Restoration – The Church should be a place where the broken find healing and wholeness.
4. Encouragement and Growth – True family challenges and strengthens one another to grow into maturity.

When sons and daughters understand their identity, they no longer live for themselves—they live to love, encourage, and strengthen others.

> *"Be devoted to one another in love. Honor one another above yourselves." – Romans 12:10 NIV*

Sons build relationships based on love and honor because they reflect the Father's heart.

Spiritual Fathers and Mothers Raise Up the Next Generation

One of the greatest needs in the Body of Christ is spiritual fathers and mothers who raise up sons and daughters in the faith.

> *"I will send you the prophet Elijah before the great and dreadful day of the Lord. He will turn the hearts of the fathers to their children, and the hearts of the children to their fathers." – Malachi 4:5-6 NIV*

The orphan spirit has led to a generation of believers who lack true fathers and mothers in the faith. Many churches operate like institutions, but sons and daughters need family.

Characteristics of Spiritual Fathers and Mothers

1. They call out identity – Just as the Father affirmed Jesus ("You are My beloved Son"), spiritual parents speak life into the next generation.
2. They create a safe environment – True fathers and mothers create a culture where people can grow without fear of rejection.
3. They lead by example – Paul said, "Follow me as I follow Christ" (1 Corinthians 11:1). Sons learn by watching fathers.
4. They pass on spiritual inheritance – A true father raises up sons to go further than he did.

Paul told the Corinthians:

"Even if you had ten thousand instructors in Christ, you do not have many fathers." – 1 Corinthians 4:15 NKJV

The Church does not need more instructors—it needs fathers and mothers who raise up sons and daughters in the faith.

The Church Is a Family, Not an Institution

Many churches today operate more like corporations than families. But Jesus never called the Church a business—He called it a family.

"You are no longer strangers and foreigners, but fellow citizens with the saints and members of God's household." –Ephesians 2:19 NKJV

How to Build a Kingdom Family in the Church

1. Make Relationship the Foundation – Programs and systems are helpful, but the core of the Church must be family and connection.

2. Create a Culture of Honor – Honor is the currency of the Kingdom. When we value each other, we create an atmosphere where sons and daughters flourish.
3. Equip and Release, Not Control – True fathers and mothers empower people rather than control them.
4. Model Servant Leadership – Jesus washed His disciples' feet. True leadership is about serving, not controlling.

"For the Son of Man did not come to be served, but to serve." –
Mark 10:45 NIV

If we truly want to see revival, we must stop building institutions and start building family.

Sons Restore the Father's Heart to the World

The greatest mission of sonship is to reveal the Father to a lost world.

"The creation waits in eager expectation for the children of God to be revealed." – Romans 8:19 NIV

This means that the world is not waiting for more religion—it is waiting for sons and daughters to rise up and reflect the Father's heart.

"If you have seen Me, you have seen the Father." – John 14:9 NKJV

Jesus revealed the Father's love everywhere He went. Now, as sons and daughters, we are called to do the same.

Sons Build the Father's Family

The Father is not looking for employees or religious servants

—He is looking for sons and daughters who will build His family on earth.

"Everything I have is yours." – Luke 15:31 NIV

When we embrace our identity as sons and daughters, we stop trying to build religious institutions and start building a family that reflects the heart of God. The world is waiting for sons and daughters to step up and bring the culture of heaven to earth. The Father is asking:

- Will you be a son or daughter who builds My house?
- Will you create a family where people can encounter My love?
- Will you be a father or mother to the next generation?

This is the call of true sonship—not just to receive the Father's love, but to give it away and build a Kingdom family that lasts for generations.

Activation Prayer

Father, I receive my calling as a son/daughter in Your family. I renounce every orphan mindset that keeps me from walking in love and honor. I declare that I will build Your Kingdom family, not religion. I will raise up sons and daughters, just as I have been raised in Your love. Let Your Church be a family where Your presence dwells. Amen.

Discussion Questions

1 . The chapter contrasts religious systems with Kingdom family. In your experience, how has the Church reflected more of an institution than a family—and what would it look like to help shift that culture toward love, honor, and connection?

2 . Why is it important for spiritual fathers and mothers to rise up in the Church today? Who has spiritually parented you, and who might God be calling you to mentor and raise up?

3 . What practical steps can you take to help build a Kingdom family in your church or community—one marked by unconditional love, servant leadership, and the Father's heart?

12

THE SPIRIT OF SONSHIP BREAKS THE ORPHAN SPIRIT

One of the greatest battles in the Kingdom is between the spirit of sonship and the orphan spirit. Ever since Adam and Eve sinned in the garden, humanity has struggled with separation from the Father. That separation created the orphan spirit—a mindset that causes people to feel rejected, unloved, and disconnected from God. But the good news is this:

"You did not receive a spirit of slavery to fall back into fear, but you received the Spirit of adoption as sons, by whom we cry, 'Abba! Father!'" – Romans 8:15 ESV

The Spirit of Sonship is the answer to the orphan spirit. When we receive our identity as sons and daughters, the orphan spirit is broken off our lives. This chapter will explore:

1. What the orphan spirit is and how it operates
2. How the Spirit of Sonship brings healing and restoration
3. How to shift from an orphan mindset to a sonship mindset

4. How to help others step into their identity as sons and daughters

What is the Orphan Spirit?

The orphan spirit is a spiritual condition that causes people to feel fatherless, abandoned, or unworthy of love. It is the root of:

- Rejection
- Insecurity
- Fear of failure
- Striving for approval
- Feeling distant from God

The first evidence of the orphan spirit was in Genesis 3, when Adam and Eve sinned. Instead of running to the Father, they hid from Him in fear. Since then, humanity has been running from the Father— trying to find love, identity, and security in other things.

"Then the man and his wife heard the sound of the Lord God as He was walking in the garden, and they hid from the Lord God among the trees." – Genesis 3:8 NIV

Signs of the Orphan Spirit

Many people love God but still operate under an orphan mindset. They believe in Jesus, but they still struggle with feelings of rejection, striving, and insecurity.

Orphan Spirit	Spirit of Sonship
Feels unworthy of love	Knows they are fully accepted
Strives for approval	Rests in the Father's love
Sees God as distant	Sees God as close and personal
Lives in fear and anxiety	Lives in peace and confidence
Seeks identity in achievements	Finds identity in relationship with the Father

The orphan spirit keeps believers trapped in a cycle of striving, but Jesus came to set us free.

The Spirit of Sonship Brings Healing

When Jesus came, He came not just to save us, but to restore us to the Father.

> *"I will not leave you as orphans; I will come to you." –John 14:18 NIV*

Jesus' mission was to bring us back into sonship. He didn't just die for our sins—He restored our relationship with the Father. Paul says:

> *"You are no longer a slave, but a son; and if a son, then an heir through God." – Galatians 4:7 ESV*

The moment we receive Jesus, we are fully restored to the Father. But for many believers, the orphan mindset remains until they receive the revelation of sonship.

How the Spirit of Sonship Heals Us

1. It restores our relationship with the Father

- We no longer see God as a distant Master—we see Him as Abba, Father.

2. It gives us a sense of belonging

- We no longer feel like outsiders—we know we are part of God's family.

3. It frees us from striving and performance

- We don't have to earn God's love—we receive it freely.

4. It replaces fear with confidence

- We no longer live in fear of rejection—we walk in boldness and peace.

"The Spirit Himself testifies with our spirit that we are children of God." – Romans 8:16 NKJV

How to Shift from an Orphan Mindset to a Sonship Mindset

The key to overcoming the orphan spirit is renewing your mind with the truth of sonship.

1. Reject the Lies of the Orphan Spirit

- The orphan spirit will tell you: "You are not good enough."
- The Father says: "You are My beloved child." (1 John 3:1)

2. Meditate on Your Identity in Christ

- Read and declare Scriptures that affirm your sonship (Romans 8:15, Galatians 4:7).
- Say daily: "I am a son/daughter of God. I am fully loved and fully accepted."

3. Spend Time in the Father's Presence

- Sons love spending time with their Father.
- The more time you spend with Him, the more you become like Him (2 Corinthians 3:18).

4. Walk in Boldness and Confidence

- Sons do not beg for favor—they walk in authority.
- Declare: "I am not an orphan. I have full access to my Father's Kingdom."

"Let us then approach God's throne of grace with confidence." –
Hebrews 4:16 NIV

Helping Others Step Into Sonship

The orphan spirit is one of the biggest barriers keeping people from experiencing true freedom in Christ. As sons and daughters of God, we are called to help others step into their identity.

How to Help Others Break Free from the Orphan Spirit

1. Call Out Their True Identity

- Speak life over them: "You are not an orphan—you are a son/daughter of God."

2. Model the Father's Love

- People don't just need to hear about God's love— they need to see it in action.
- Show unconditional love and honor.

3. Pray for the Spirit of Sonship to Be Released

- Lay hands on them and pray for freedom from the orphan mindset.

4. Teach Them to Hear the Father's Voice

- Help them develop a personal relationship with the Father.
- Encourage them to listen to His voice and meditate on His Word.

"The creation waits in eager expectation for the children of God to be revealed." – Romans 8:19 NIV

The world is waiting for sons and daughters to rise up in their true identity.

The Orphan Spirit Has No Power Over You

The enemy wants to keep you stuck in an orphan mindset, but Jesus came to break every chain and restore you to sonship.

"I will be a Father to you, and you will be My sons and daughters." – 2 Corinthians 6:18 NIV

You are not abandoned. You are not rejected. You are not forgotten. You are a beloved son or daughter, fully accepted and fully empowered to walk in your inheritance. The Father is saying:

"You are always with Me, and everything I have is yours." – Luke 15:31 NIV

It's time to walk in your identity as a son/daughter of God.

Activation Prayer

Father, I renounce the orphan spirit and every lie that tells me I am not worthy. I receive my identity as Your beloved child. I declare that I am fully loved, fully accepted, and fully empowered. I will walk in the Spirit of Sonship and help others do the same. I am a son/daughter of the King. Amen.

Discussion Questions

1. In what ways have you personally experienced or recognized the orphan spirit in your life—through fear, striving, or insecurity? How has the revelation of sonship begun to heal and transform those areas?

2. The chapter teaches that the orphan mindset isn't always broken immediately, even after salvation. What does it look like to daily renew your mind in the truth of your identity as a son or daughter of God?

3. How can you help others around you—friends, family, or those in your church—step out of the orphan spirit and into the Spirit of Sonship? What are some practical ways to model the Father's love?

13

THE FATHER'S DISCIPLINE
SON'S ARE TRAINED, NOT PUNISHED

One of the greatest misunderstandings in the Church today is how the Father disciplines His children. Many believers confuse discipline with punishment, thinking that God is angry or disappointed when they fail. But in the Kingdom, discipline is not about rejection—it is about training and growth.

"The Lord disciplines the one He loves, and He chastens everyone He accepts as His son." – Hebrews 12:6 NIV

Just as a loving father trains his children, God disciplines us so that we can mature as sons and daughters. This chapter will explore:

- The difference between punishment and discipline
- Why discipline is a sign of sonship
- How the Father corrects us with love and grace
- How to embrace discipline and grow into maturity

The Difference Between Punishment and Discipline

Many believers think that when they sin or fail, God punishes them in anger. But the Bible is clear:

"There is no condemnation for those who are in Christ Jesus."
Romans 8:1 NIV

Punishment vs. Discipline

Punishment (Orphan Mindset)	Discipline (Sonship Mindset)
Rooted in anger and rejection	Rooted in love and relationship
Designed to make you pay for your mistake	Designed to make you grow from your mistake
Leads to shame and fear	Leads to freedom and wisdom
Creates distance from God	Brings us closer to the Father

God does not punish His children—He trains them. When we fail, the Father does not say, "I am done with you." Instead, He says, "Let's learn from this and grow."

Discipline is a Sign of Sonship

The Bible tells us that God disciplines those He loves:

"If you are not disciplined—and everyone undergoes discipline— then you are not legitimate, not true sons and daughters at all." –
Hebrews 12:8 NIV

This means that discipline is not rejection—it is proof of sonship. A father does not discipline someone else's child—he disciplines his own child because he loves them and wants the best for them. If God never corrected us, it would mean we are not truly His children. But because we are His sons and daughters, He teaches us, corrects us, and helps us grow.

How the Father Disciplines Us with Love and Grace

When God disciplines us, it is always in love, never in anger.

"For the Lord disciplines those He loves, just as a father disciplines the son in whom he delights." – Proverbs 3:12 NIV

Ways the Father Disciplines Us

1. Through His Word – The Bible guides and corrects us (2 Timothy 3:16).
2. Through Conviction of the Holy Spirit – The Spirit gently corrects us (John 16:8).
3. Through Life Lessons – God allows challenges to shape our character (Romans 5:3-4).
4. Through Spiritual Leaders – He uses pastors and mentors to guide us (Proverbs 27:17).
5. Through Inner Growth – Sometimes, discipline is God teaching us patience, humility, or endurance.

God does not use sickness, accidents, or disaster to discipline us. He is a good Father who corrects us with love, not harm.

"His kindness leads us to repentance." – Romans 2:4 NIV

How to Embrace Discipline and Grow into Maturity

Discipline is not something to fear—it is something to embrace.

"No discipline seems pleasant at the time, but later it produces a harvest of righteousness and peace for those who have been trained by it." – Hebrews 12:11 NIV

How to Respond to the Father's Discipline

1. Trust His Heart – Remember, God's discipline is always for your good (Romans 8:28).
2. Don't Resist Correction – Be open to learning and growing (Proverbs 12:1).
3. Stay Close to the Father – When corrected, run to God, not away from Him (James 4:8).
4. Learn the Lesson – Ask: "Father, what do You want to teach me through this?"
5. Move Forward in Maturity – Don't dwell on past mistakes; learn and grow (Philippians 3:13-14).

Sons do not fear discipline—they embrace it because they know it is shaping them for greatness.

"Endure hardship as discipline; God is treating you as His children." – Hebrews 12:7 NIV

Sons Are Trained for Greater Authority

One of the biggest reasons God disciplines His sons and daughters is because He is preparing them for greater responsibility.

"Those who are faithful with little will be entrusted with much." – Luke 16:10 NIV

God does not just want to bless us—He wants us to carry His authority with maturity. Biblical Examples of Sons Who Were Trained Through Discipline

1. Joseph – Before he ruled Egypt, he endured years of testing and refining (Genesis 37-50).
2. Moses – Before leading Israel, he spent 40 years in the wilderness being prepared (Exodus 3-4).

3. David – Before becoming king, he was trained in hardship, betrayal, and waiting (1 Samuel 16-30).
4. Jesus Himself – Even Jesus "learned obedience through what He suffered" (Hebrews 5:8).

God trains sons not to harm them, but to prepare them for their Kingdom calling.

"The whole creation waits in eager expectation for the sons of God to be revealed." – Romans 8:19 NIV

Sons who have been trained by the Father will be entrusted with greater things.

Discipline is the Mark of True Sons

Many people fear discipline, thinking it is a sign of God's anger. But the truth is, discipline is proof that you are loved and chosen. The Father is saying: "You are My son. I am shaping you for something greater." You are not being punished—you are being prepared. The world is waiting for mature sons and daughters to rise up in strength, wisdom, and authority. The question is:

- Will you embrace the Father's training?
- Will you allow Him to shape you into a mature son/daughter?
- Will you trust that His discipline is always for your good?

When you understand that discipline is love, you will embrace the process and grow into the fullness of your calling.

"For those whom the Lord loves He disciplines." –Hebrews 12:6 ESV

Activation Prayer

Father, I thank You that I am Your son/daughter. I choose to embrace Your discipline as training, not punishment. I reject every orphan mindset that makes me fear correction. I trust Your heart and Your wisdom. Shape me into the mature son/daughter You have called me to be. I will walk in obedience, wisdom, and authority. Amen.

Discussion Questions

1. Why do you think so many believers confuse discipline with punishment? How does understanding the Father's heart help you receive correction as a sign of love rather than rejection?

2. This chapter says, "Sons do not fear discipline—they embrace it." What is one area in your life where you've recently experienced God's correction or growth? How did it shape you?

3. Hebrews 12:7 says to "endure hardship as discipline." How can a shift in mindset—seeing life's challenges as training for greater authority—transform the way you respond to adversity?

14

SONS LIVE IN REST, NOT STRIVING

One of the biggest differences between an orphan spirit and a spirit of sonship is how we relate to work, success, and rest. Orphans strive—they feel like they must prove their worth through their achievements, performance, and busyness. They believe that if they can just do enough, they will finally be accepted and secure. Sons, however, live from a place of rest. They know that they are already fully loved, fully accepted, and fully secure in the Father's love. They do not have to earn their place— they simply receive what has already been given to them.

"Come to Me, all you who are weary and burdened, and I will give you rest." – Matthew 11:28 NIV

In this chapter, we will explore:

1. Why the orphan spirit leads to striving and burnout
2. How true sons live from rest, not pressure
3. Why rest is the foundation of supernatural power
4. How to shift from a mindset of striving to a mindset of sonship

The Orphan Spirit Strives for Approval

One of the signs of an orphan spirit is the constant need to perform, achieve, and prove oneself. Many believers unconsciously think:

- "If I just do more, God will love me more."
- "If I succeed, then I will be valuable."
- "If I work harder, I will finally have peace."

But this is a lie. No amount of performance, hard work, or success can earn what the Father has already freely given. Jesus warned against this mindset when He spoke to Martha:

"Martha, Martha, you are worried and upset about many things, but only one thing is needed. Mary has chosen what is better." –
Luke 10:41-42 NIV

Martha was striving in service, while Mary was resting in relationship. Sons do not live in pressure—they live in peace.

True Sons Work From Rest, Not for Rest

Many people believe that if they work hard enough, they will eventually reach a place of rest. But in the Kingdom, rest is not a reward—it is the starting place. "It is finished." – John 19:30Jesus already accomplished everything on the cross. We are not working to earn sonship—we are working from sonship.

The Difference Between Orphan Work and Sonship Work

Orphan Mindset	Sonship Mindset
Works for approval	Works from approval
Driven by fear of failure	Motivated by love and purpose
Finds identity in achievements	Finds identity in relationship with the father
Rest is a luxury	Rest is a lifestyle

Sons are not lazy—they still work, serve, and build the Kingdom. But they do it from a place of security, not striving.

"Unless the Lord builds the house, the builders labor in vain." –
Psalm 127:1 NIV

When sons build from rest, they build with the Father's strength, not their own.

Rest is the Foundation of Supernatural Power

One of the most overlooked secrets of supernatural power is resting in God's presence. Jesus lived in constant miracles, but He never rushed or worked in pressure and anxiety. He often withdrew to be alone with the Father:

"Jesus often withdrew to lonely places and prayed." – Luke
5:16 NIV

Resting in the Father's presence is what empowered Jesus to:

- Heal the sick
- Multiply food
- Calm storms
- Cast out demons effortlessly

Because He operated from the Father's love, He never burned out or became overwhelmed. The secret to walking in supernatural power is not working harder—it's resting deeper.

"Be still, and know that I am God." – Psalm 46:10 NIV

Sons understand that power flows from rest.

How to Shift from Striving to Sonship

If you have lived in a mindset of striving, the Father is inviting you to step into His rest.

1. Break Agreement with the Lie That You Have to Earn Love

- The orphan spirit whispers: "You must work for approval."
- The Father says: "You are already fully loved." Declare: "I am loved, accepted, and secure in my Father's love."

2. Stop Measuring Your Worth by Your Performance

- You are not valuable because of what you do—you are valuable because of who you are.
- Your identity is not in your success, ministry, or reputation—it is in being a child of God.

3. Spend Time in the Father's Presence Daily

- Sons prioritize being with the Father over working for Him.
- Spend time in prayer, worship, and stillness—not as a duty, but as a joy. "Draw near to God, and He will draw near to you." – James 4:8

4. Work from Rest, Not for Rest

- Rest is not the absence of work—it is working from a place of peace.
- When you feel stressed or overwhelmed, stop and return to the Father's presence.

5. Trust the Father's Timing and Provision

- Sons do not rush or force things—they trust the Father's provision and perfect timing.
- Declare: "I will not strive—I will trust.""In repentance and rest is your salvation, in quietness and trust is your strength." – Isaiah 30:15

Sons Live in the Sabbath Rest of God

Many people think the Sabbath is just about one day of rest, but in the Kingdom, the Sabbath is a lifestyle.

"There remains a Sabbath rest for the people of God, for anyone who enters God's rest also rests from their works, just as God did from His." – Hebrews 4:9-10 NIV

True sons live in perpetual rest, because they trust in the finished work of Jesus.

"Come to Me, all you who are weary and burdened, and I will give you rest." – Matthew 11:28 NIV

When we embrace the Father's rest, we live in:

- Peace instead of pressure
- Confidence instead of insecurity
- Joy instead of burnout
- Power instead of exhaustion

This is the freedom of sonship.

Sons Rest Because They Trust the Father

The Father is inviting you to lay down striving and step into His perfect rest. You do not have to prove yourself. You do not have to earn His love. You do not have to carry the pressure of success on your own. You are a beloved son/daughter, and your Father is pleased with you—not because of what you do, but because of who you are. The Father is saying: "Be still, My child. Rest in My love. Everything I have is already yours."

Activation Prayer

Father, I renounce the orphan spirit and the mindset of striving. I receive the Spirit of Sonship, and I step into Your rest. I trust that I am fully loved and fully accepted. I refuse to measure my worth by my performance. I will live in peace, confidence, and supernatural rest. Amen.

Discussion Questions

1. Why do you think so many believers—especially in today's culture—struggle with striving and burnout? How does the orphan spirit contribute to this cycle of performance?

2. The chapter says, "Rest is not a reward—it's the starting place." What does it practically look like for you to live and work from rest rather than for rest in your current season?

3. What mindset shifts or daily practices can help you break free from performance-based identity and embrace the peace, joy, and power that come from resting as a son or daughter of the Father?

15

SONS LIVE IN RADICAL GENEROSITY

One of the greatest marks of a true son or daughter of God is a heart of radical generosity. Orphans fear lack, so they hold on tightly to their resources. They believe that if they give too much, they won't have enough for themselves. But sons trust the Father's provision and know that everything they have comes from Him.

"My son, you are always with Me, and everything I have is yours."
– Luke 15:31 NIV

Sons do not live with a scarcity mindset—they live with an abundance mindset. This chapter will explore:

1. How sonship shifts us from a poverty mindset to an abundance mindset
2. Why generosity is the natural overflow of knowing the Father's love
3. How giving unlocks supernatural provision
4. How to walk in radical generosity as a lifestyle

The Orphan Mindset vs. The Sonship Mindset in Provision

The orphan spirit creates a poverty mentality—the belief that there is not enough and that we must strive, hoard, or compete to survive. This is why some believers struggle to give—deep down, they fear that if they let go, they won't have enough. But Jesus taught a completely different way of thinking:

"Give, and it will be given to you. A good measure, pressed down, shaken together and running over, will be poured into your lap." – Luke 6:38 NIV

Sons do not fear giving—they know that the Father is their source, not their job, salary, or savings.

The Difference Between an Orphan Mindset and a Sonship Mindset

Orphan Mindset	Sonship Mindset
Thinks resources are limited	Knows the father's supply is endless
Hoards out of fear of lack	Gives freely, trusting the father
Believes blessing is earned	Knows blessing is inherited
Lives with scarcity thinking	Lives with abundance thinking
Always worried about money	Walks in peace and provision

Jesus said:

"So do not worry, saying, 'What shall we eat? What shall we drink? What shall we wear?'... Your heavenly Father knows that you need them." – Matthew 6:31-32 NIV

Orphans worry about resources—sons rest in the Father's provision.

True Sons Live to Give, Not Just Receive

Many people pray, "God, bless me." But sons pray, "God, make me a blessing."

Jesus said:

"It is more blessed to give than to receive." – Acts 20:35 ESV

The Father is generous, and when we walk in sonship, His generosity flows through us.

Why Sons Give Freely

1. Because the Father is Generous – "For God so loved the world that He gave." (John 3:16)
2. Because Giving is an Act of Trust – Giving shows that we trust God, not money.
3. Because Generosity Unlocks Blessing – "Whoever sows generously will also reap generously." (2 Corinthians 9:6)
4. Because We Are Called to Represent the Father – Sons are called to reflect the generosity of their Father. Generosity is not just about money—it is about a way of life. "Freely you have received; freely give." – Matthew 10:8

Giving Unlocks Supernatural Provision

Many believers struggle with finances because they have never stepped into the principle of Kingdom generosity. Jesus said:

"Give, and it will be given to you... running over." – Luke 6:38 NIV

The world says, "Hold onto what you have." The Kingdom says, "Give, and watch God multiply it."

Biblical Examples of Radical Giving Unlocking Provision

1. The Widow at Zarephath (1 Kings 17:8-16)

- She gave her last meal to Elijah, and God supernaturally provided for her during the famine.

2. The Boy with Five Loaves and Two Fish (John 6:9-13)

- He gave his small lunch, and Jesus multiplied it to feed thousands.

3. The Macedonian Church (2 Corinthians 8:1-4)

- Even in poverty, they gave generously, and God blessed them abundantly.

When we give, we are inviting the Father to become our provider.

"And my God will supply all your needs according to His riches in glory." – Philippians 4:19 NKJV

Sons do not rely on the economy—they rely on the Father's economy.

How to Walk in Radical Generosity

If you want to live as a true son or daughter, you must step into a lifestyle of generosity.

1. See Yourself as a Steward, Not an Owner

- Everything you have belongs to the Father.

- You are managing His resources, not your own.

2. Give First, Not Last

- Sons make giving their first priority, not an afterthought.
- The Bible teaches the principle of firstfruits—giving to God before anything else (Proverbs 3:9).

3. Give Beyond Money

- Generosity is not just about tithing—it's about living with open hands.
- Give your time, encouragement, and resources freely.

4. Give Without Fear

- The enemy wants you to fear lack, but the Father wants you to trust His provision.
- Declare: "I am a son/daughter. My Father provides for me, and I have more than enough to give."

5. Expect Harvest from Your Giving

- Sons do not give just to get, but they also expect harvest because God's Word promises it (Galatians 6:9).
- When you give, expect supernatural provision to follow. "Whoever sows generously will also reap generously." – 2 Corinthians 9:6

Sons Reflect the Generosity of the Father

A true son does not just receive the Father's love—he becomes a reflection of it. The Father is radically generous, and when we live in sonship, we become radically generous too. Jesus said:

"Freely you have received; freely give." – Matthew 10:8 NKJV

This means:

- We give because we are loved, not to earn love.
- We give because we trust the Father, not because we fear lack.
- We give because we know that when we pour out, He fills us back up.

The world is waiting for sons and daughters who will reflect the Father's generosity.

"The creation waits in eager expectation for the children of God to be revealed." – Romans 8:19 NIV

When we step into radical generosity, we show the world who our Father is.

Sons Are Generous Because They Are Secure

Sons and daughters do not hold back in fear—they give freely in faith. The Father is saying:

"Everything I have is yours. Trust Me, and live with open hands."

When you live in sonship:

- You stop worrying about provision.
- You become a blessing to others.
- You walk in supernatural abundance.

The orphan spirit says, "Hold on, or you won't have enough." The Father says, "Give, and watch Me pour out more than enough." This is the freedom of sonship.

Activation Prayer

Father, I break agreement with the orphan spirit and every fear of lack. I receive my identity as a son/daughter in Your Kingdom. I trust that You are my Provider, and I will never lack. I choose to live with open hands and radical generosity. Let my life be a reflection of Your heart of abundance. Amen.

Discussion Questions

1. Why do you think fear of lack is so common among believers, even though Jesus promises that the Father will provide? How does the orphan mindset feed into that fear, and how can sonship break it?

2. This chapter says, "True sons live to give, not just to receive." How can you begin to shift your mindset and lifestyle toward radical generosity—not just with money, but with your time, resources, and relationships?

3. The chapter lists several biblical examples where radical giving led to supernatural provision. Have you ever experienced or witnessed that kind of breakthrough through generosity? What keeps people from giving freely, and how can you overcome that?

16

SON'S WALK IN AUTHORITY AND DOMINION

One of the greatest truths of sonship is that sons and daughters of God have been given authority to rule and reign in the earth. Orphans live under circumstances, but sons govern circumstances. Orphans pray weak prayers, but sons decree and declare. Orphans fear the enemy, but sons exercise dominion over him. Jesus didn't just come to save us—He came to restore our authority.

"Behold, I have given you authority to tread on serpents and scorpions, and over all the power of the enemy, and nothing shall harm you." – Luke 10:19 ESV

In this chapter, we will explore:

1. How Jesus restored dominion to sons and daughters
2. The difference between praying as an orphan and praying as a son
3. How to exercise Kingdom authority in every area of life
4. How to walk in dominion over the enemy

Jesus Restored Our Lost Authority

When God created mankind, He gave them dominion:

"God said, 'Let Us make mankind in Our image... so that they may rule over the fish in the sea, the birds in the sky, the livestock, and all the creatures that move along the ground.'" – Genesis 1:26 NIV

Adam and Eve were not created as servants or slaves—they were created as royalty. They were designed to govern the earth as God's representatives. But when Adam and Eve sinned, they lost their authority, and the enemy took dominion over the world. This is why Satan is called the 'prince of this world' (John 12:31). However, Jesus came to take back the authority that was lost:

"All authority in heaven and on earth has been given to Me." – Matthew 28:18 NIV

And then He gave that authority to us:

"I have given you authority to trample on snakes and scorpions and to overcome all the power of the enemy." – Luke 10:19 NIV

Through Christ, dominion has been restored to sons and daughters.

Sons Decree – Orphans Beg

One of the greatest differences between an orphan mindset and a sonship mindset is how we pray and speak. Orphans pray weak, uncertain prayers:

- "God, please do something."
- "I hope You answer me."
- "I don't know if I have the power to do this."

Sons pray with authority:

- "In Jesus' name, I command this to be done."
- "I have the authority to speak life and change circumstances."
- "I declare that heaven's will is done on earth."

The Difference Between Orphan Prayer and Sonship Prayer

Orphan Prayers	Sonship Decrees
Asks God to do everything	Exercises authority as a son
Hopes God answers	Knows they have power in Jesus' name
Begging prayers	Commanding prayers
Focuses on problems	Speaks solutions

Jesus didn't say to beg God for miracles—He said to command them:

"Heal the sick, raise the dead, cleanse the lepers, cast out demons. Freely you have received; freely give." – Matthew 10:8 NKJV

Sons command things to align with the will of the Father.

How to Exercise Kingdom Authority

Authority is not something you earn—it is something you inherit as a son or daughter. But many believers fail to walk in it because they do not understand how to use it. Steps to Walking in Kingdom Authority

1. Speak with Boldness and Confidence

- Jesus never begged for a miracle—He spoke with authority.
- When He healed the sick, He said, "Be healed."

- When He cast out demons, He said, "Come out!"
- Sons and daughters speak with the same confidence.

2. Align Your Words with Heaven

- Your words have power (Proverbs 18:21).
- Do not speak fear, doubt, or unbelief—speak faith, life, and truth.
- Declare: "I am a son/daughter of God, and I have been given authority."
- "I decree that the will of the Father is done in my life."

3. Exercise Dominion Over Your Circumstances

- If Jesus could speak to storms, then so can you (Mark 4:39).
- If Jesus could command sickness to leave, then so can you (Luke 10:9).
- If Jesus had authority over lack, then so do you (Matthew 14:19-20).

Sons do not accept circumstances—they change them.

Walking in Dominion Over the Enemy

The orphan spirit fears the devil, but sons rule over him.

"Submit yourselves to God. Resist the devil, and he will flee from you." – James 4:7 NIV

Sons do not fear demons—they cast them out. Sons do not run from spiritual attacks—they take authority over them. Jesus said:

"In My name, they will drive out demons." – Mark 16:17 NIV

How to Walk in Dominion Over the Enemy

1. Know That You Have Authority – The devil only has power when you believe his lies (Luke 10:19).
2. Use the Name of Jesus – Demons must submit to the name of Jesus (Philippians 2:10).
3. Speak the Word of God – Jesus defeated Satan by declaring Scripture (Matthew 4:4-10).
4. Live in Holiness – A life of righteousness keeps you protected from the enemy's attacks (Ephesians 6:10-18).

Sons do not live in fear of darkness—they bring the light of the Kingdom wherever they go.

"The creation waits in eager expectation for the children of God to be revealed." – Romans 8:19 NIV

The world is waiting for sons and daughters to rise up and walk in their full authority.

Sons Establish the Kingdom on Earth

Jesus did not tell us to wait for heaven—He told us to bring heaven to earth:

"Your Kingdom come, Your will be done, on earth as it is in heaven." – Matthew 6:10 NKJV

Sons are not just called to pray for change—they are called to create change.

How Sons Establish the Kingdom

- In Their Families – Bringing peace, love, and leadership to their homes.
- In Their Communities – Shifting the atmosphere with the Father's love.
- In Their Workplaces – Carrying Kingdom values into business, education, and government.
- In Their Churches – Raising up disciples who know their authority.

The Father is looking for sons and daughters who will bring heaven to earth.

"Fear not, little flock, for it is your Father's good pleasure to give you the Kingdom." – Luke 12:32 NKJV

Sons Walk in Power, Not Fear

The Father is saying: "You are My son. You are My daughter. I have given you authority—now go and use it." You are not powerless. You are not weak. You are not at the mercy of the enemy. You have been given the same authority that Jesus walked in. The time to walk in dominion is now.

Activation Prayer

Father, I receive my authority as a son/daughter in Your Kingdom. I renounce every orphan mindset that keeps me powerless. I declare that I walk in boldness, power, and dominion. I will speak with authority, pray with confidence, and bring heaven to earth. The enemy has no power over me—I rule and reign as Your child. Amen.

Discussion Questions

1. This chapter contrasts orphan prayers with sonship decrees. How have you seen these two approaches play out in your own prayer life? What might shift if you began praying more like a son or daughter with authority?

2. What are some practical ways you can exercise Kingdom authority in your everyday circumstances—at home, at work, in your community, or in spiritual warfare?

3. Jesus didn't just save us; He restored our dominion. In what areas of life have you been living under your circumstances instead of ruling over them—and how can you begin to take your rightful place as a son or daughter who governs with confidence?

17

SONS WALK IN INTIMACY WITH THE HOLY SPIRIT

One of the greatest gifts given to sons and daughters of God is the Holy Spirit. The Holy Spirit is not just a force or a power—He is the Spirit of the Father, living within us. He is the seal of our sonship, the comforter, the teacher, and the empowerer who enables us to walk in our full inheritance as children of God.

"The Spirit you received does not make you slaves, so that you live in fear again; rather, the Spirit you received brought about your adoption to sonship. And by Him we cry, 'Abba, Father.'" – Romans 8:15 NIV

This chapter will explore:

1. How the Holy Spirit confirms our identity as sons and daughters
2. The role of the Holy Spirit in guiding and teaching us
3. How to develop a deep, daily relationship with the Holy Spirit
4. How the Holy Spirit empowers us to walk in supernatural power

The Holy Spirit Confirms Our Sonship

One of the most powerful truths of the New Covenant is that the Holy Spirit is the guarantee of our sonship.

"The Spirit Himself testifies with our spirit that we are God's children." – Romans 8:16 NIV

This means that when we receive the Holy Spirit, He reminds us daily that we belong to the Father. What Happens When the Holy Spirit Confirms Our Sonship?

1. We walk in confidence, not insecurity.

- We no longer question if God loves or accepts us.

2. We hear the Father's voice clearly.

- The Holy Spirit helps us recognize and trust the Father's voice (John 10:27).

3. We develop a deeper intimacy with God.

- The Holy Spirit draws us closer into relationship with the Father (John 16:13-14).

4. We are no longer driven by fear.

- Fear is broken because the Holy Spirit reminds us that we are sons and daughters, not orphans (2 Timothy 1:7).

Sons and daughters do not wonder if they belong—they know they do because the Spirit of the Father lives within them.

The Holy Spirit is Our Teacher and Guide

Jesus told His disciples that the Holy Spirit would come to teach and guide them:

"But the Advocate, the Holy Spirit, whom the Father will send in My name, will teach you all things and will remind you of everything I have said to you." – John 14:26 NIV

This means that as sons and daughters, we do not have to walk through life confused, unsure, or lost. The Holy Spirit is our constant guide, leading us in the wisdom and revelation of the Father.

How the Holy Spirit Teaches and Guides Us

1. Through the Word of God – He illuminates Scripture and gives revelation and understanding (John 16:13).
2. Through the Inner Witness – He speaks to our hearts, leading us in the right direction (Romans 8:14).
3. Through Prophetic Insight – He gives dreams, visions, and prophetic words to direct our steps (Acts 2:17).
4. Through Conviction, Not Condemnation – He gently corrects us, leading us back to the Father's heart (John 16:8).

Jesus said:

"When He, the Spirit of truth, comes, He will guide you into all truth." – John 16:13 NIV

Sons and daughters trust the Holy Spirit's leading because they know that He is always pointing them to the Father.

Developing Daily Intimacy with the Holy Spirit

Many believers know about the Holy Spirit, but few walk in daily relationship with Him. The Holy Spirit is not just for church services or spiritual moments—He desires to be with us in every part of our lives.

"Do you not know that your body is a temple of the Holy Spirit, who is in you, whom you have received from God?" – 1 Corinthians 6:19 NIV

Practical Ways to Grow in Intimacy with the Holy Spirit

1. Invite Him Into Your Daily Life

- Begin your day with: "Holy Spirit, I welcome You. Lead me, guide me, and speak to me today."

2. Spend Time in His Presence

- Worship is one of the greatest ways to encounter the Holy Spirit (Psalm 22:3).

3. Pray in the Spirit

- Praying in tongues builds up your spirit and connection with God (1 Corinthians 14:4).

4. Be Sensitive to His Voice

- The Holy Spirit speaks in whispers, impressions, and leadings—learn to recognize His voice.

5. Obey His Promptings

- The more we obey the Holy Spirit, the stronger our relationship with Him becomes.

Sons and daughters are not just aware of the Holy Spirit—they walk in deep fellowship with Him every day.

The Holy Spirit Empowers Sons to Walk in Supernatural Power

Jesus promised that when the Holy Spirit came, we would receive power:

> *"You will receive power when the Holy Spirit comes upon you, and you will be My witnesses." – Acts 1:8 NIV*

The Holy Spirit does not just give us comfort and guidance—He gives us supernatural power to advance the Kingdom.

Ways the Holy Spirit Empowers Sons and Daughters

1. Power to Heal the Sick – Sons and daughters lay hands on the sick, and they recover (Mark 16:18).
2. Power to Cast Out Demons – Sons have authority over the enemy (Luke 10:19).
3. Power to Prophesy – The Holy Spirit releases divine insight and revelation (Acts 2:17-18).
4. Power to Boldly Preach the Gospel – Sons are not ashamed of the Good News (Acts 4:31).
5. Power to Demonstrate the Kingdom – Miracles, signs, and wonders follow those who walk in the Spirit (1 Corinthians 2:4-5)."The Kingdom of God is not a matter of talk but of power." – 1 Corinthians 4:20

Sons and daughters do not just talk about the Kingdom—they demonstrate it through the power of the Holy Spirit.

Walking in the Spirit as a Lifestyle

Walking in the Holy Spirit is not a one-time experience—it is a lifestyle of continual fellowship with Him. Paul gives us this command:

"Walk by the Spirit, and you will not gratify the desires of the flesh."
– Galatians 5:16 NIV

This means that everything we do—how we think, how we act, how we speak—should be led by the Holy Spirit.

How to Walk in the Spirit Daily

1. Start Your Day in the Spirit

- Begin every morning with prayer, worship, and Scripture.

2. Stay Aware of His Presence Throughout the Day

- Check in with the Holy Spirit often: "Holy Spirit, what are You saying?"

3. Listen and Obey Promptings Quickly

- When you feel the Holy Spirit leading you to pray for someone, encourage someone, or take action—obey!

4. Live a Life of Holiness

- Sons and daughters walk in purity and righteousness because they carry the presence of God. "If we live by the Spirit, let us also keep in step with the Spirit." – Galatians 5:25

The Holy Spirit is not just for special moments—He is for every moment.

Sons Live in Fellowship with the Holy Spirit

The Father never intended for His sons and daughters to live life alone—He gave us His Spirit to guide, comfort, and empower us. You are not abandoned. You are not powerless. You are a son or daughter, filled with the Spirit of God. The Father is saying: "Walk with My Spirit. Listen to His voice. He will lead you into your full inheritance."

Activation Prayer

Father, I thank You for the gift of the Holy Spirit. I receive His presence, guidance, and power in my life. I choose to walk in deep fellowship with Him daily. I will listen, obey, and move in supernatural power. I am a son/daughter of the Kingdom, led by the Spirit of God. Amen.

Discussion Questions

1 . How does the Holy Spirit confirm your identity as a son or daughter of God in your daily life? Have you experienced moments when His voice or presence reassured you of your belonging?

2 . The chapter lists ways the Holy Spirit teaches, guides, and empowers us. Which of these have you personally experienced, and which would you like to grow in more deeply?

3 . What practical changes can you make in your daily routine to develop greater intimacy with the Holy Spirit and live a lifestyle of walking in the Spirit, not just occasional encounters?

18

SONS WALK IN THEIR FULL INHERITANCE

One of the greatest truths about sonship is that sons and daughters of God are heirs. Everything that belongs to the Father belongs to His children. We are not just servants or followers—we are heirs of God's Kingdom.

"The Spirit Himself testifies with our spirit that we are children of God. And if children, then heirs—heirs of God and co-heirs with Christ." – Romans 8:16-17 NIV

An orphan mentality makes believers feel unworthy to receive the fullness of what the Father has given them. But when we understand that we are heirs, we step into our full inheritance and live in the abundance of God's Kingdom. This chapter will explore:

1. What it means to be an heir of God
2. How inheritance is received, not earned
3. The spiritual and natural blessings of sonship
4. How to walk in your full inheritance today

What It Means to Be an Heir of God

When a person is an heir, it means they are entitled to receive what belongs to their father. In the natural world, children inherit everything their parents own. This is exactly what Jesus taught about our relationship with God:

"Fear not, little flock, for it is your Father's good pleasure to give you the Kingdom." – Luke 12:32 NKJV

Everything that belongs to the Father now belongs to us. Paul makes this even clearer:

"For all things are yours, whether Paul or Apollos or Cephas or the world or life or death or the present or the future—all are yours, and you are Christ's, and Christ is God's." – 1 Corinthians 3:21-23 ESV

Sons and daughters are not spiritual beggars—they are heirs of an abundant Kingdom.

Inheritance is Received, Not Earned

One of the biggest mistakes believers make is thinking that they must work for their inheritance. But the truth is:

- Inheritance is not based on performance.
- Inheritance is not earned by effort.
- Inheritance is given simply because you are a son or daughter.

"For by grace you have been saved through faith, and this is not from yourselves; it is the gift of God." – Ephesians 2:8 NIV

You don't have to strive for what already belongs to you.

The Orphan Mindset vs. The Sonship Mindset in Inheritance

Orphan Mentality	Sonship Mentality
"I must work for what I receive"	"I receive because I am an heir"
"I don't deserve God's blessings"	"My father freely gives me all things"
"I hope God answers my prayers"	"I have access to my inheritance now"
"I must earn God's love and favor"	"I already have God's love and favor"

Sons don't fight for their inheritance—they receive it by faith.

The Spiritual and Natural Blessings of Sonship

Many believers only think of spiritual blessings, but the Bible is clear: God's inheritance includes both spiritual and natural provision.

Spiritual Inheritance

1. The Father's Love – Sons live in constant love and acceptance (Romans 8:15).
2. Supernatural Authority – Sons have authority over sickness, demons, and circumstances (Luke 10:19).
3. Direct Access to God – Sons can boldly approach the Father at any time (Hebrews 4:16).
4. Eternal Life and Glory – Sons inherit the Kingdom for eternity (Revelation 21:7).

Natural Inheritance

1. Provision and Prosperity – Sons never lack because the Father is their provider (Philippians 4:19).
2. Favor and Open Doors – Sons walk in divine opportunities (Psalm 5:12).
3. Divine Protection – Sons are covered and guarded (Psalm 91:1-4).

4. Legacy and Multiplication – Sons leave a blessing for generations (Proverbs 13:22).

God's inheritance is not limited to heaven—it is meant to be experienced on earth as well.

"Your Kingdom come, Your will be done, on earth as it is in heaven." – Matthew 6:10 NKJV

How to Walk in Your Full Inheritance Today

Many believers are waiting to receive their inheritance, but the truth is: You already have it!

"His divine power has given us everything we need for life and godliness." – 2 Peter 1:3 NIV

Steps to Walking in Your Full Inheritance

1. Believe That You Are an Heir

- If you don't believe you have an inheritance, you won't walk in it.
- Declare: "I am an heir of God and co-heir with Christ."

2. Renew Your Mind with the Truth of Sonship

- Meditate on Romans 8:15-17 and Ephesians 1:3-14.
- Replace orphan thinking with Kingdom thinking.

3. Stop Striving and Start Receiving

- You don't have to beg for what is already yours.

- Pray with confidence, knowing that the Father has already provided.

4. Walk in Faith and Expectation

- Sons expect favor, blessing, and supernatural provision.
- Declare: "Everything I need has already been given to me."

5. Release Your Inheritance to Others

- Your inheritance is not just for you—it is meant to bless others.
- As you walk in your fullness, help others step into theirs.

"Freely you have received; freely give." – Matthew 10:8 NKJV

Sons Live as Kings, Not Beggars

One of the greatest tragedies in the Church today is that many believers live as spiritual beggars when they are called to be kings and queens in God's Kingdom.

"To the one who overcomes, I will give the right to sit with Me on My throne." – Revelation 3:21 NIV

Sons and daughters rule and reign with Christ. They:

- Walk in confidence and boldness
- Speak with authority
- Expect favor and supernatural provision
- Operate in Kingdom dominion

The world is waiting for sons and daughters to step into their full inheritance.

"The creation waits in eager expectation for the children of God to be revealed." – Romans 8:19 NIV

The question is:

- Will you live in the fullness of your inheritance?
- Will you receive what the Father has already given?
- Will you stop striving and start reigning as a son or daughter?

The time to walk in your inheritance is now.

You Have Already Been Given Everything

The Father is saying:

"You are always with Me, and everything I have is yours." – Luke 15:31 NIV

You are not waiting for an inheritance—you are already an heir. You are not a spiritual beggar—you are a ruler in the Kingdom. You are not fighting for victory—you are walking from victory. It's time to live in the fullness of your inheritance as a son or daughter of God.

Activation Prayer

Father, I receive my inheritance as Your son/daughter. I reject every orphan mindset that tells me I am not worthy. I declare that I am an heir of Your Kingdom. I walk in supernatural provision, authority, and blessing. Everything You have is mine, and I will use it for Your glory. Amen.

Discussion Questions

1. What mindsets or beliefs have kept you from receiving your full inheritance as a son or daughter of God? How can you begin to replace those with Kingdom thinking?

2. The chapter outlines both spiritual and natural inheritance. Which part of your inheritance do you need to more fully embrace—spiritual authority, provision, favor, legacy, etc.?

3. What does it practically look like to stop striving and start receiving? How can you begin living today as a king or queen in God's Kingdom rather than as a spiritual beggar?

19

SONS LIVE WITH A KINGDOM LEGACY MINDSET

One of the greatest revelations of sonship is that sons and daughters do not live just for themselves—they live to leave a legacy that advances the Father's Kingdom for generations to come. Orphans live only for the present—they focus on survival, temporary success, and short-term impact. Sons and daughters, however, think generationally—they build, invest, and disciple in ways that outlive them.

"A good man leaves an inheritance to his children's children." –
Proverbs 13:22 NKJV

In this chapter, we will explore:

1. Why sons and daughters think generationally
2. The difference between temporary success and Kingdom legacy
3. How to leave a spiritual inheritance for future generations
4. How to live today with an eternal impact in mind

Sons Think Generationally

The Bible is filled with stories of how God works through generations. "I am the God of Abraham, Isaac, and Jacob." – Exodus 3:6 God's promise to Abraham was not just for him—it was for his descendants:

"I will make you into a great nation, and I will bless you... and all peoples on earth will be blessed through you." – Genesis 12:2-3 NIV

Orphans vs. Sons in How They See Legacy

Orphan Mindset	Sonship Mindset
Focuses on personal success	Focuses on Kingdom impact
Thinks only about today	Thinks about generations to come
Seeks temporary fulfillment	Builds for eternal impact
Wants to keep success to themselves	Invests in raising others up

Sons understand that their lives are part of a bigger story. They do not just seek personal blessings—they live in a way that ensures the next generation receives even more.

Temporary Success vs. Kingdom Legacy

The world tells us that success is measured by personal achievements—how much we own, how much we accomplish, and how far we go. But in the Kingdom, true success is measured by what we build that lasts beyond us. "Only one life, 'twill soon be past, only what's done for Christ will last." – C.T. Studd

The Difference Between Temporary Success and Kingdom Legacy

Temporary Success	Kingdom Legacy
Measured by personal achievements	Measured by impact on others
Fades when we die	Lasts for generations
Focuses on what we receive	Focuses on what we give
Built through personal effort	Built through obedience to God

Jesus never pursued temporary success—He pursued Kingdom impact. He lived His life investing in others, raising up disciples who would continue His work after He left.

"Go and make disciples of all nations." – Matthew 28:19 NIV

Sons and daughters understand that their greatest success is not in what they accomplish, but in what they pass on to others.

Leaving a Spiritual Inheritance for Future Generations

A true legacy is not just about money or possessions—it is about leaving a spiritual inheritance that impacts generations after us.

"The righteous will be remembered forever." – Psalm 112:6 NIV

How to Leave a Kingdom Legacy

1. Disciple and Mentor Others

- Sons do not just grow in their faith—they help others grow too.
- Jesus spent His life raising disciples who carried His legacy forward.

2. Build Something That Outlives You

- Invest in ministries, churches, and Kingdom initiatives that will impact generations.
- What you build today should continue to bear fruit long after you're gone.

3. Raise Up Sons and Daughters in the Faith

- Paul told Timothy: "What you have heard from me, entrust to faithful men who will teach others." (2 Timothy 2:2)
- Sons think beyond themselves—they raise up the next generation.

4. Live a Life of Integrity and Faithfulness

- Your character is part of your legacy—people will remember your faith, not just your achievements.
- Walk in obedience to the Father, so your life becomes a testimony that inspires others.

5. Give Generously to the Next Generation

- Sons and daughters invest their time, wisdom, and resources into the next generation.
- Legacy is not just about what you receive—it is about what you give away.

Living Today with an Eternal Impact in Mind

Many people think about the future but fail to live today with eternity in mind.

"Do not store up for yourselves treasures on earth... but store up for yourselves treasures in heaven." – Matthew 6:19-20 NIV

Jesus taught that everything we do should be for eternal impact, not temporary gain.

How to Live Every Day with a Kingdom Legacy Mindset

1. Ask: "What I am building—will it last?"

- Is your focus on earthly things or eternal things?
- Are you investing in things that will outlive you?

2. Make Every Decision with Future Generations in Mind

- Every choice you make impacts those who come after you.
- Sons and daughters think about the bigger picture.

3. Teach, Lead, and Impart What You've Learned

- If God has taught you something, pass it on to others.
- What you impart to others today will grow into a greater harvest tomorrow.

4. Invest in People, Not Just Projects

- Legacy is not just about what you build—it's about who you invest in.
- Jesus' greatest legacy was not the miracles He did— it was the disciples He raised up.

"What you have heard from me, entrust to faithful men who will teach others." – 2 Timothy 2:2 ESV

Sons do not just chase personal success—they build something that will last for eternity.

Sons Build for the Next Generation

One of the greatest examples of building for the next generation is King David. David had a dream to build a temple for God, but God told him that his son, Solomon, would build it instead.

"Your son Solomon will build the house for My Name." – 1 Kings 5:5 NIV

Instead of being disappointed, David spent his life preparing everything Solomon needed to build the temple.

- He gathered gold, silver, and materials.
- He gave Solomon wisdom and leadership guidance.
- He made sure that the next generation had everything they needed.

David understood that his greatest legacy was not in what he did, but in what he prepared for the next generation to accomplish.

Sons Build for Those Who Come After Them

- They don't just think about their lifetime—they prepare for generations to come.
- They don't seek personal success—they raise up spiritual sons and daughters.
- They don't hold onto everything—they give freely, knowing that what they give will multiply.

The world is waiting for sons and daughters to build something that lasts.

"The creation waits in eager expectation for the children of God to be revealed." – Romans 8:19 NIV

Sons Live for Kingdom Legacy

The Father is saying: "Build something that will outlive you. Raise up the next generation. Leave a Kingdom legacy." You were not made just to succeed for yourself—you were made to impact generations. You were not made to just receive—you were made to impart and give away. It's time to think beyond today and start living for eternity.

Activation Prayer

*Father, I receive my calling to live with a Kingdom legacy mindset.
I reject the orphan mindset that seeks only temporary success. I will
invest in the next generation and leave an inheritance that will last.
Let my life be a testimony of faith, wisdom, and obedience. I choose
to build for Your Kingdom, not just for myself. Amen.*

Discussion Questions

1. What's the difference between building personal success and building a Kingdom legacy? In what areas of your life have you been focused more on the temporary than the eternal?

2. Who are you currently investing in, mentoring, or discipling that could carry your spiritual legacy forward? What steps can you take to be more intentional about raising up the next generation?

3. King David prepared resources for Solomon to build what he could not. What can you begin building, gathering, or sowing today to empower future generations for Kingdom impact?

20

SONS REIGN WITH THE FATHER

The final and ultimate revelation of sonship is that sons and daughters are not just servants or followers—they are co-heirs, kings, and priests, called to reign with the Father. Jesus did not just come to rescue us from sin—He came to restore our dominion and authority. Sons and daughters of God are not victims of this world—they are called to govern, establish the Kingdom, and walk in rulership with the Father.

"To the one who overcomes, I will give the right to sit with Me on My throne, just as I overcame and sat down with My Father on His throne." – Revelation 3:21 NIV

This chapter will explore:

- How Jesus restored our right to reign
- Why sons and daughters are called to rule in life
- How to walk in spiritual kingship and priesthood
- What it means to reign with Christ for eternity

Jesus Restored Our Right to Reign

When God created Adam and Eve, He gave them dominion over the earth:

"Let Us make mankind in Our image... so that they may rule over all the earth." – *Genesis 1:26 NIV*

However, when Adam and Eve sinned, they lost their authority, and the enemy took dominion. This is why the Bible calls Satan "the god of this world" (2 Corinthians 4:4). But Jesus came to take back everything that was lost.

"All authority in heaven and on earth has been given to Me." – *Matthew 28:18 NIV*

And then He gave that authority back to us:

"You have made them to be a kingdom and priests to serve our God, and they will reign on the earth." – *Revelation 5:10 NIV*

Through Christ, our original dominion and rulership have been restored.

Sons and Daughters Are Called to Rule in Life

The Bible does not say we should wait for heaven to walk in authority—it says we are called to reign in life now.

"Those who receive the abundance of grace and the gift of righteousness will reign in life through the One, Jesus Christ." – *Romans 5:17 NKJV*

What Does It Mean to Reign in Life?

1. Reigning Over Fear and Anxiety

- Sons and daughters do not live in fear—they walk in perfect peace (Isaiah 26:3).

2. Reigning Over Sin and Temptation

- We are no longer slaves to sin—we are masters over it (Romans 6:14).

3. Reigning Over Sickness and Weakness

- Sons walk in divine health and healing (Mark 16:17-18).

4. Reigning Over Lack and Poverty

- Sons know that their Father provides for all their needs (Philippians 4:19).

5. Reigning Over Circumstances

- Sons do not react to life's challenges—they speak to them and shift atmospheres (Mark 11:23).

Sons and daughters are not under circumstances—they rule over them.

Walking in Kingship and Priesthood

The Bible says we are called to be kings and priests:

"You are a chosen people, a royal priesthood, a holy nation, God's special possession." – 1 Peter 2:9 NIV

What Does It Mean to Be a King and a Priest?

- As Kings, We Rule and Establish God's Kingdom
- We have been given authority and dominion over the earth (Luke 10:19).
- We bring Kingdom order into chaos.
- As Priests, We Represent God to the World
- We are called to bring heaven to earth (Matthew 6:10).
- We intercede for nations, families, and the lost.

How to Walk in Your Kingship and Priesthood

1. Declare Your Authority Daily

- Speak the Word of God with power and confidence.
- Declare: "I am a king and a priest, ruling with my Father."

2. Walk in Righteousness and Boldness

- Kings do not act like slaves—they walk in dignity and confidence.
- Priests carry holiness and the presence of God.

3. Use Your Authority to Shift Atmospheres

- Speak peace where there is fear.
- Speak healing where there is sickness.
- Speak life where there is darkness.

Sons do not beg for breakthrough—they speak it into existence.

"You shall decree a thing, and it shall be established for you." – Job 22:28 NKJV

Reigning with Christ for Eternity

Our sonship is not just for this life—we are called to reign with Christ forever.

"If we endure, we will also reign with Him." – 2 Timothy 2:12 ESV

The Bible teaches that Jesus is coming back, and when He does, He will establish His Kingdom fully on the earth.

"The kingdom of the world has become the Kingdom of our Lord and of His Messiah, and He will reign forever and ever." – Revelation 11:15 NIV

When that happens, we will:

- Rule and reign with Christ over nations (Revelation 2:26).
- Sit with Jesus on His throne (Revelation 3:21).
- Judge angels and govern in the Kingdom (1 Corinthians 6:3).

Our time on earth is training for the eternal Kingdom.

Sons Establish the Father's Kingdom on Earth

Jesus did not tell us to wait for heaven—He told us to bring heaven to earth.

"Your Kingdom come, Your will be done, on earth as it is in heaven." – Matthew 6:10 NKJV

How to Establish the Father's Kingdom on Earth

1. Live with a Kingdom Mindset

- Think and act like a son or daughter of a King.

2. Speak with Authority

- Decree and declare God's will over your life and circumstances.

3. Transform Culture

- Bring Kingdom principles into your workplace, family, and community.

4. Raise Up Other Sons and Daughters

- Disciple and mentor others into their Kingdom identity.

The world is waiting for sons and daughters to rise up and establish God's rule on the earth.

"The creation waits in eager expectation for the children of God to be revealed." – Romans 8:19 NIV

The Father is looking for sons and daughters who will rule and reign with Him. The question is:

- Will you step into your full authority?
- Will you live as a king and a priest?
- Will you establish the Father's Kingdom on earth?

The time to reign is now.

You Were Made to Reign

The Father is saying: "You are My son. You are My daughter. I have given you dominion—now walk in it." You are not a slave—you are a king and a priest. You are not powerless—you have authority in Christ. You are not waiting for victory—you are walking from victory. It's time to step into your royal identity and reign with the Father.

Activation Prayer

*Father, I receive my identity as a king and priest in Your Kingdom.
I renounce every orphan mindset that keeps me powerless. I declare
that I reign in life through Jesus Christ. I will establish Your
Kingdom on earth as it is in heaven. I am seated with Christ in
heavenly places. I walk in boldness, power, and dominion. Amen.*

Discussion Questions

1 . What does it practically look like for you to live as both a
king and a priest in your everyday life? In what areas are you
currently walking in dominion, and where might God be calling
you to rise up in greater authority?

2 . How does knowing that you are seated with Christ and
called to reign in life shift the way you approach fear, temptation, lack, or opposition?

3 . What are some specific ways you can begin to establish
God's Kingdom in your family, workplace, or community
this week?

21

THE MANIFESTATION OF SONS
REVEALING THE FATHER TO THE WORLD

One of the greatest purposes of sonship is that sons and daughters reveal the Father to the world. Jesus did not come just to show us how to live—He came to reveal the heart of the Father. Now, as sons and daughters, we are called to continue that mission.

"If you have seen Me, you have seen the Father." – John 14:9 NIV

The world is not waiting for more religion—it is waiting for sons and daughters to manifest and reveal the Father's love.

"The creation waits in eager expectation for the children of God to be revealed." – Romans 8:19 NIV

This chapter will explore:

1. Why the world is waiting for sons and daughters to rise up
2. How sons manifest the love, power, and character of the Father

3. How to live as a visible representation of the Father on earth
4. How to bring transformation through the revelation of sonship

The World is Waiting for Sons to Rise Up

The Bible says that creation itself is groaning for sons and daughters to be revealed.

"The creation waits with eager longing for the revealing of the sons of God." – Romans 8:19 ESV

Why? Because when sons and daughters walk in their full identity:

- They bring the presence of the Father into every place they go.
- They heal, restore, and release the Kingdom of heaven on earth.
- They show the world what the Father looks like.

Jesus was the perfect manifestation of sonship, and now, He has called us to do the same:

"As the Father has sent Me, I am sending you." – John 20:21 NIV

Sons and daughters do not live passive Christian lives—they actively reveal the Father in everything they do.

How Sons Manifest the Father on Earth

Jesus said: "I only do what I see My Father doing." – John 5:19 Everything Jesus did—healing the sick, forgiving sinners, loving the outcasts, casting out demons—was a reflection of the Father's heart.

Ways Sons Manifest the Father

1. Through Love and Compassion

- Sons and daughters love the unlovable because they have received the Father's love.
- "By this everyone will know that you are My disciples, if you love one another." – John 13:35

2. Through Supernatural Power

- Jesus healed the sick and cast out demons because He was revealing the Father's power to restore.
- "Whoever believes in Me will do the works I have been doing, and they will do even greater things." – John 14:12

3. Through Boldness and Authority

- Sons do not walk in timidity—they walk in confidence because they know who their Father is.
- "The righteous are bold as a lion." – Proverbs 28:1

4. Through Holiness and Righteousness

- The Father is holy, and His sons and daughters reflect His purity and righteousness.
- "Be holy, because I am holy." – 1 Peter 1:16

5. Through Servant Leadership

- Sons and daughters serve others because they carry the heart of the Father.
- "For even the Son of Man did not come to be served, but to serve." – Mark 10:45

The more we become like Jesus, the more we reveal the Father to the world.

Living as a Visible Representation of the Father

Many people talk about God, but few truly reveal Him through their lives. Jesus did not say, "If you hear Me, you hear the Father." He said, "If you have seen Me, you have seen the Father." The world needs to see the Father in us.

How to Represent the Father Well

1. Walk in Intimacy with Him

- The closer you are to the Father, the more you will reflect His heart.
- Spend time in prayer, worship, and the Word daily.

2. Carry His Presence Everywhere You Go

- Sons and daughters bring the atmosphere of heaven into every room they enter.
- Walk with an awareness of the Holy Spirit living in you.

3. Live as a Peacemaker and Healer

- The Father is a healer and a reconciler—we are called to do the same.

- Be a person who brings peace, unity, and healing to broken places.

4. Operate in Miracles, Signs, and Wonders

- Sons and daughters demonstrate the power of the Kingdom.
- Pray for healing, speak life over people, and expect supernatural breakthroughs.

5. Speak Life and Truth

- The Father's words bring life—our words should do the same.
- Declare blessings, not curses over people and situations.

The world should be able to look at us and see the Father.

"Let your light shine before others, that they may see your good deeds and glorify your Father in heaven." – Matthew 5:16 NIV

Sons Bring Transformation Through Revelation

When sons and daughters walk in the revelation of who they are, they transform the world around them.

"The Kingdom of God is not a matter of talk but of power." – 1 Corinthians 4:20 NIV

True sonship is not just about personal identity—it is about bringing heaven's culture to earth.

How Sons Bring Transformation

1. They Change Atmospheres

- When sons and daughters walk into a room, the spiritual atmosphere shifts.
- They carry the presence and peace of the Father.

2. They Set People Free

- Sons cast out fear, break strongholds, and release the freedom of Christ.
- "Where the Spirit of the Lord is, there is freedom." – 2 Corinthians 3:17

3. They Release Kingdom Solutions

- Sons and daughters carry divine wisdom for business, education, government, and culture.
- "You will be called priests of the Lord; you will be named ministers of our God." – Isaiah 61:6

4. They Make Disciples

- Sons raise up other sons.
- Jesus' final command was to make disciples of all nations (Matthew 28:19).

The greatest revival in history will come when sons and daughters rise up and fully manifest the Father's heart on earth.

The Time for Sons to Manifest is Now

The world is waiting. Creation is groaning. The Father is calling His sons and daughters to rise up.

"You are the light of the world." – Matthew 5:14 NKJV

This is not a future promise—it is a present calling.

- Will you rise up as a son or daughter?
- Will you reveal the Father in your life?
- Will you bring heaven to earth?

The time is now.

You Are the Father's Representative on Earth

The Father is saying: "My child, the world is waiting for you to rise up. You are My son. You are My daughter. Go and reveal My heart to the world." You are not just a believer—you are a manifestation of the Father's love. You are not just a follower of Jesus—you are sent as He was sent. You are not just waiting for heaven—you are called to bring heaven to earth. It's time to manifest your sonship and reveal the Father.

Activation Prayer

Father, I receive my calling to manifest Your heart on the earth. I renounce every orphan mindset that keeps me hidden. I declare that I will walk as a true son/daughter of Your Kingdom. Let my life reveal Your love, power, and glory. I am ready to bring heaven to earth. Amen.

Discussion Questions

1. In what ways can your daily life—your words, actions, and relationships—more clearly reveal the heart of the Father to those around you?

2. What aspects of Jesus' life and ministry do you feel most challenged to reflect in your own sonship? (e.g., love, supernatural power, boldness, servant leadership)

3. The world is "waiting for the sons of God to be revealed." What would it look like for you to fully manifest your identity as a son or daughter in your workplace, family, or community right now?

22

SONS WALK IN UNSHAKABLE IDENTITY

One of the greatest weapons the enemy uses against believers is identity confusion. If the enemy can make you question who you are, he can keep you from walking in the fullness of your sonship. From the very beginning, Satan's strategy has been to attack identity. In the Garden of Eden, he deceived Eve by making her question what God had said. In the wilderness, he tempted Jesus by saying, "If you are the Son of God..." (Matthew 4:3). But true sons and daughters of God walk in unshakable identity. They do not let circumstances, people, or even their own feelings determine their worth. They stand firm in the truth:

"See what great love the Father has lavished on us, that we should be called children of God! And that is what we are!" – 1 John 3:1 NIV

This chapter will explore:

1. How identity is the foundation of everything in the Kingdom
2. Why the enemy attacks your identity and how to overcome it

3. How to live in unshakable confidence as a son or daughter of God
4. Practical ways to strengthen your identity daily

Identity is the Foundation of the Kingdom

Everything in the Kingdom of God flows from identity. Before you can fully walk in authority, dominion, or purpose, you must first know who you are. Jesus did not begin His ministry until the Father declared His identity:

"This is My beloved Son, in whom I am well pleased." – Matthew 3:17 NKJV

Before Jesus performed a single miracle, the Father affirmed Him as a Son, fully loved and accepted. This is the foundation of sonship:

- You are not working for love—you are working from love.
- You are not trying to prove yourself—you are already chosen.
- You do not need to earn favor—you already have it.

Why Identity is Key

1. Identity Defines Your Authority – You cannot walk in authority if you do not know you have it.
2. Identity Determines Your Confidence – Sons walk in boldness because they know they are fully accepted.
3. Identity Protects You from Deception – The enemy cannot deceive someone who is secure in their identity. If you do not know who you are, the world will try to define you.

The Enemy Attacks Your Identity First

The devil knows that if he can confuse your identity, he can keep you from fulfilling your purpose. This is why, immediately after the Father declared, "This is My beloved Son", the enemy attacked Jesus' identity in the wilderness:

"If You are the Son of God, tell these stones to become bread." –
Matthew 4:3 NIV

Satan knew Jesus was the Son of God, but he wanted Jesus to doubt it. He used the same tactic in the Garden of Eden: "Did God really say...?" – Genesis 3:1 Satan always attacks identity because identity determines destiny.

Ways the Enemy Attacks Identity

1. Through Lies and Accusations

- The enemy whispers: "You're not good enough. You're not really chosen. You don't belong."
- But the Father says: "You are My beloved child."

2. Through Circumstances

- When life is hard, the enemy says: "If God really loved you, why is this happening?"
- But the Father says: "I will never leave you nor forsake you."

3. Through the Opinions of Others

- The world tries to define you by your mistakes, background, or failures.

- But the Father says: "I have called you by name; you are Mine." – Isaiah 43:1

If the enemy cannot change who you are, he will try to make you forget who you are.

How to Live in Unshakable Confidence as a Son or Daughter

Sons and daughters do not live based on feelings or circumstances—they live based on the unchanging truth of God's Word.

"Heaven and earth will pass away, but My words will never pass away." – Matthew 24:35 NIV

Keys to Walking in Unshakable Identity

1. Root Your Identity in the Word, Not in Feelings

- Feelings change, but the truth of who you are never changes.
- Speak this daily: "I am a child of God. I am fully loved and fully accepted."

2. Reject Every Lie That Contradicts Your Identity

- Whenever a thought comes that challenges your identity, reject it immediately.
- Declare: "I take every thought captive to make it obedient to Christ." – 2 Corinthians 10:5

3. Live from the Father's Affirmation, Not People's Approval

- Sons and daughters do not seek validation from others—they know they are already accepted.

- Stop looking for identity in achievements, relationships, or status—your identity comes from the Father.

4. Speak and Declare Your Identity Daily

- Your words shape your mindset.
- Every morning, declare: "I am a child of God, chosen and set apart. I am fully loved, fully accepted, and fully empowered."

5. Walk in Boldness and Authority

- Sons do not shrink back in fear—they step forward with confidence.
- "The righteous are bold as a lion." – Proverbs 28:1

When you know who you are, nothing can shake you.

Practical Ways to Strengthen Your Identity Daily

Sonship is not just a belief—it must be a daily reality in your life.

Daily Practices to Strengthen Your Identity

1. Spend Time in the Father's Presence

- The more time you spend with the Father, the more you know who you are.
- Prioritize prayer, worship, and the Word.

2. Surround Yourself with Kingdom-Minded People

- Community matters—surround yourself with people who remind you of your identity.
- "As iron sharpens iron, so one person sharpens another." – Proverbs 27:17

3. Renew Your Mind Daily

- Meditate on Scriptures about sonship and identity.
- Read Romans 8, Ephesians 1, and Galatians 4 often.

4. Guard Against Identity Theft

- Be mindful of anything that tries to redefine you—whether it's culture, social media, or personal failures.
- Filter everything through the Word of God.

5. Step Into Your Calling Boldly

- Sons and daughters walk in purpose without fear.
- Do not wait until you "feel ready"—move forward in faith.

The World Needs Sons Who Know Who They Are

The world is desperate for authentic sons and daughters who walk in confidence and authority.

"The creation waits in eager expectation for the children of God to be revealed." – Romans 8:19 NIV

Sons and daughters who know their identity:

- Do not waver in trials
- Do not live in fear or insecurity
- Do not question their worth or calling

- Do not need approval from man

The world is waiting for you to rise up. Will you step into your true identity today?

You Are Unshakable

The Father is saying: "You are My beloved child, and I am well pleased with you". You are not what the world says you are—you are who the Father says you are. You are not defined by your past —you are defined by your sonship. You are not a slave, not an orphan, not forgotten—you are a chosen heir of God.

Now, walk in unshakable identity.

Activation Prayer

*Father, I receive my identity as Your beloved son/daughter. I
renounce every lie of the enemy that tries to define me. I declare that
I am fully loved, fully accepted, and fully empowered. I walk in
confidence, boldness, and Kingdom authority. I am unshakable
because my identity is in You. Amen.*

Discussion Questions

1. Why do you think the enemy attacks identity first—and
how have you personally experienced this in your own
journey of faith?

2. Which lies about your identity have you had to (or still need
to) confront and replace with God's truth? What Scriptures
anchor your true identity?

3. What daily habits or practices help you stay rooted in your
identity as a son or daughter of God, especially during times
of hardship or doubt?

23

SONS WALK IN THE FULLNESS OF
THEIR CALLING

One of the greatest privileges of sonship is that every son
and daughter has a divine calling and purpose. You were
not created by accident. You were sent to this earth for a Kingdom
assignment. Many believers struggle with the question:

- "What is my purpose?"
- "How do I know what I am called to do?"
- "How do I walk in the fullness of my calling?"

The answer is found in sonship. Sons and daughters of God
do not strive to find purpose—they discover it by walking with
the Father.

*"For we are His workmanship, created in Christ Jesus for good
works, which God prepared beforehand that we should walk in
them." – Ephesians 2:10 NKJV*

This chapter will explore:

1. How your calling is rooted in sonship, not
   performance

2. How to recognize your divine assignment
3. How to overcome fear and step boldly into your purpose
4. How to walk in the fullness of your calling daily

Your Calling is Rooted in Sonship, Not Performance

Many people believe that their calling is something they must earn—but in the Kingdom, calling is an inheritance, not a reward.

"Before I formed you in the womb, I knew you, and before you were born, I set you apart." – Jeremiah 1:5 NIV

Your calling was not given based on your qualifications—it was given before you were even born.

The Difference Between Orphan Calling and Sonship Calling

Orphan Mindset	Kingdom Legacy
"I need to prove myself to be used by God"	"I am chosen, and my calling is a gift from the father"
"I don't know if I have what it takes"	"I have everything I need in Christ"
"I must work for favor and anointing"	"I receive my calling through grace, not works"

Sons and daughters do not chase purpose—they walk in purpose by being close to the Father.

"He who abides in Me, and I in him, bears much fruit." – John 15:5 NKJV

The more you abide in the Father, the more your calling naturally unfolds.

Recognizing Your Divine Assignment

Every son and daughter of God has a unique assignment—a specific way they are called to advance the Kingdom.

"We have different gifts, according to the grace given to each of us."
– Romans 12:6 NIV

How to Recognize Your Calling

1. Pay Attention to What Stirs Your Heart

- What burdens you? What excites you?
- Your passion is often a clue to your assignment.

2. Look at Your Gifts and Strengths

- God has given you natural and spiritual gifts for your purpose.
- Ask: "What am I naturally good at?"

3. Ask the Father to Show You

- Sons do not figure out their calling alone—they ask the Father.
- Pray: "Father, reveal the assignment You have placed on my life."

4. Be Faithful in Small Assignments

- Your purpose unfolds as you walk in obedience daily.
- Jesus said: "Whoever is faithful with little will be entrusted with much." – Luke 16:10

Your calling is not a mystery—the Father wants you to walk in it more than you do.

Overcoming Fear and Stepping Into Purpose

Many believers never walk in their calling because they allow fear, doubt, or comparison to hold them back.

"For God has not given us a spirit of fear, but of power, love, and a sound mind." – 2 Timothy 1:7 NKJV

Common Lies That Stop People From Walking in Their Calling

1. "I'm not qualified."

- The Father doesn't call the qualified—He qualifies the called.
- "Not by might, nor by power, but by My Spirit." – Zechariah 4:6

2. "What if I fail?"

- Sons do not fear failure because they know their Father walks with them.
- "I will never leave you nor forsake you." – Hebrews 13:5

3. "What if people reject me?"

- Jesus was rejected by man but chosen by the Father.
- "If God is for us, who can be against us?" – Romans 8:31

4. "I don't have enough resources."

- Sons trust in the Father's provision, not their own resources.

- "My God will supply all your needs." – Philippians 4:19

Fear is a trap that keeps sons from stepping into purpose. But the truth is: Your calling is bigger than your fears. "The righteous are bold as a lion." – Proverbs 28:1

Walking in the Fullness of Your Calling Daily

Sonship is not just about knowing your calling—it is about walking in it every day.

"Walk worthy of the calling you have received." –Ephesians 4:1 NIV

Practical Steps to Walk in Your Calling

1. Start Where You Are

- Do not wait for a perfect moment—step out in faith now.
- Ask: "What can I do today to walk in my calling?"

2. Say Yes to Small Assignments

- Every great purpose starts with obedience in small things.
- Faithfulness in small things prepares you for greater things.

3. Speak Life Over Your Calling

- Declare: "I am called, anointed, and empowered for my Kingdom assignment."
- Your words shape your reality (Proverbs 18:21).

4. Surround Yourself with Kingdom-Minded People

- Who you walk with will either push you toward or away from your calling.
- Walk with those who encourage and strengthen your faith.

5. Trust the Father's Timing

- Sons do not force doors open—they trust the Father's timing.
- "At the right time, I, the Lord, will make it happen." – Isaiah 60:22

The more you walk in obedience, the more your purpose unfolds.

Your Calling is Bigger Than You

Many believers think their calling is just about them—but true sons and daughters know their calling is about advancing the Kingdom and impacting others.

"Freely you have received; freely give." – Matthew 10:8 NKJV

Sons and daughters understand that their purpose is part of a bigger story.

- Moses' calling was not just for him—it was to lead Israel to freedom.
- Esther's calling was not just for her—it was to save an entire nation.
- Paul's calling was not just for him—it was to bring the Gospel to the world.

Your calling is bigger than you—it is part of God's plan for generations to come.

Step Into Your Kingdom Assignment

The Father is saying:"I have called you. I have chosen you. Now step forward in boldness." You are not forgotten—you were sent here with a purpose. You are not insignificant—your calling has eternal impact. You are not waiting for a purpose—you are already called. It's time to step into the fullness of your assignment.

Activation Prayer

Father, I receive my calling as Your son/daughter. I renounce fear, doubt, and hesitation. I declare that I am chosen, anointed, and empowered. I will walk boldly in my Kingdom assignment. I trust Your timing, Your provision, and Your leading. I step into my purpose today. Amen.

Discussion Questions

1. In what ways does understanding your identity as a son or daughter of God change how you view your purpose and calling?

2. What fears or lies have you had to confront—or still need to confront—that are holding you back from walking fully in your Kingdom assignment?

3. What practical steps can you take this week to walk more boldly and faithfully in the purpose God has placed on your life?

24

SONS CARRY THE FATHER'S HEART FOR THE NATIONS

One of the greatest aspects of sonship is that sons and daughters carry the heart of the Father for the world. The Father's love is not limited to one group of people—it is for every tribe, tongue, and nation. When sons and daughters walk in their true identity, they begin to see the world through the Father's eyes and carry His burden for the nations.

"Ask of Me, and I will give You the nations as Your inheritance, the ends of the earth as Your possession." – Psalm 2:8 NKJV

Jesus came to reveal that the Father's love is for all people. As sons and daughters, we are called to extend His love, grace, and Kingdom to the ends of the earth.

This chapter will explore:

1. How the Father's heart beats for the nations
2. Why sons and daughters are called to bring the Kingdom to all people
3. How to develop a global Kingdom mindset

4. Practical ways to partner with the Father in reaching the world

The Father's Heart for the Nations

From the beginning, the Father's desire was that all nations would know Him.

"It is too small a thing for You to be My servant to restore the tribes of Jacob. I will also make You a light for the nations, that My salvation may reach the ends of the earth." - Isaiah 49:6 NIV

When God called Abraham, He didn't just promise to bless him—He promised to bless all nations through him:

"Through your offspring, all nations on earth will be blessed." - Genesis 22:18 NIV

This promise was fulfilled through Jesus, and now, as His sons and daughters, we are part of that same mission to bless the nations.

Sons and Daughters are Called to Bring the Kingdom to All People

Jesus' final command before He ascended to heaven was not just for a small group—it was a global assignment: "Go and make disciples of all nations." – Matthew 28:19 Sons and daughters do not just think about their own lives—they live with a Kingdom mindset that includes the nations.

Why Sons and Daughters Are Called to the Nations

1. The Father Desires All People to Know Him

- "God so loved the world that He gave His one and only Son." – John 3:16
- Sons and daughters are ambassadors of the Father's love to all people.

2. The Harvest is Ready

- "The harvest is plentiful, but the workers are few." – Matthew 9:37
- The world is hungering for the love of the Father.

3. We Are Blessed to Be a Blessing

- Sons and daughters do not keep their inheritance to themselves—they release it to others.
- "Freely you have received; freely give." – Matthew 10:8

4. Every Nation is Part of God's Family

- Heaven will be filled with people from every tribe and tongue (Revelation 7:9).
- Sons and daughters bring heaven's culture to earth by embracing all people.

Developing a Global Kingdom Mindset

Sons and daughters do not just think locally—they think globally. They understand that their assignment is bigger than their city, country, or personal world.

How to Develop a Global Kingdom Mindset

1. Pray for the Nations

- The Father's heart burns for the nations—ours should too.
- Ask: "Father, which nation do You want me to intercede for?"

2. Learn About Other Cultures

- Sons and daughters seek to understand different people groups.
- Ask the Father to give you compassion for nations you do not know.

3. Support Global Missions and Ministries

- Not everyone is called to travel, but everyone is called to support the work of the Kingdom.
- Find ways to give, serve, and encourage those on the mission field.

4. Ask the Father to Expand Your Vision

- Pray: "Father, show me where You are moving in the nations. Let me be part of Your global plan."
- Sons and daughters do not limit their vision—they dream with the Father for the nations.

Practical Ways to Partner with the Father in Reaching the World

The Father is always looking for sons and daughters who will partner with Him to bring His love to the world. "Here I am. Send me." – Isaiah 6:8

How You Can Be Part of the Father's Global Mission

1. Pray for the Nations Regularly

- Set aside time to intercede for different regions of the world.

2. Support Kingdom Work Financially

- Invest in ministries that spread the Gospel and help the poor.
- Giving is part of your inheritance as a son or daughter.

3. Engage with International Communities Locally

- Many nations are represented in your own city.
- Befriend people from different backgrounds and share the Father's love.

4. Consider Going on a Mission Trip

- Ask the Father if you are called to go to the nations physically.
- Even a short-term trip can change your perspective and impact lives.

5. Use Your Gifts to Serve Globally

- Your talents (business, teaching, arts, technology) can be used to advance the Kingdom in nations.

The Father has given every son and daughter a role in bringing His love to the world.

The Time to Act is Now

Jesus said:

"This Gospel of the Kingdom will be preached in the whole world as a testimony to all nations, and then the end will come." – Matthew 24:14 NIV

The world is waiting for sons and daughters to rise up and bring the Kingdom to every nation.

The Father is asking:

- Will you carry My heart for the nations?
- Will you pray, give, go, and support My mission on earth?
- Will you see beyond your own life and step into My global plan?

The time is now—sons and daughters must take their place in God's story for the nations.

You Are Called to Impact the Nations

The Father is saying: "My child, My heart burns for the nations. I have given you a place in My global mission. Step forward and carry My love to the world." You are not just called for your city—you are called for the nations. You are not just here to receive blessings—you are here to bless the world. You are not waiting for revival—you are part of bringing it to the earth. It's time to carry the Father's heart for the nations.

Activation Prayer

Father, I receive Your heart for the nations. I declare that I am a son/daughter sent to reveal Your love to the world. I renounce every small mindset and step into a global Kingdom vision. I will pray, give, go, and support Your mission on earth. Here I am, Lord—send me. Amen.

Discussion Questions

1. What does it mean to you personally that the Father's love is for every tribe, tongue, and nation—and how does this challenge your current worldview or comfort zone?

2. In what ways can you begin to develop a more global Kingdom mindset in your daily life, even if you never leave your city?

3. How might the Father be inviting you to partner with Him —through prayer, giving, going, or serving—to bring His love and Kingdom to the nations?

25

THE SPIRIT OF SONSHIP BRINGS REVIVAL

Throughout history, every great move of God has been marked by intimacy with the Father. True revival is not just about signs, wonders, and miracles—it is about sons and daughters returning to the heart of the Father and leading others into the same revelation. The Spirit of Sonship is the key to revival. When the Church moves from an orphan mindset to a sonship mindset, it shifts from striving to resting in the Father's love, from religious duty to authentic relationship, and from fear to boldness and authority.

"In the last days, I will pour out My Spirit on all people; your sons and daughters will prophesy." – Joel 2:28 NIV

This chapter will explore:

1. Why true revival starts with the revelation of sonship
2. How the Spirit of Sonship breaks religious bondage and brings freedom
3. The role of sons and daughters in carrying revival to the world
4. How to sustain revival through a culture of sonship

Revival Begins with the Revelation of Sonship

Many people pray for revival, but true revival begins with the heart of the Father. Jesus' mission was not just to perform miracles—it was to reveal the Father and restore sonship:

"I have made Your name known to them, and will continue to make it known, so that the love You have for Me may be in them." – John 17:26 NIV

When people encounter the Father's love, they experience:

- Healing from the orphan spirit
- Freedom from religious striving
- An identity that cannot be shaken

Revival is not just about an outpouring of the Holy Spirit—it is about sons and daughters stepping into their inheritance and transforming the world.

"Creation waits in eager expectation for the children of God to be revealed." – Romans 8:19 NIV

The Spirit of Sonship Breaks Religious Bondage and Brings Freedom

One of the biggest enemies of revival is the spirit of religion—a mindset that focuses on rules, performance, and striving instead of relationship and intimacy with the Father. Jesus came to destroy religious bondage and restore sonship:

"You will know the truth, and the truth will set you free." – John 8:32 NIV

The Difference Between Religious Bondage and Sonship Revival

Religious Bondage	Spirit of Sonship Revival
Strives to earn God's approval	Lives in the father's unconditional love
Sees God as a distant judge	Sees God as an intimate father
Motivated by fear and duty	Motivated by love and relationship
Trapped in tradition	Moves in supernatural freedom
Operates in works	Operates in grace

The spirit of religion kills revival, but the Spirit of Sonship releases it.

Sons and Daughters Are Called to Carry Revival to the World

True revival does not just happen inside churches—it happens when sons and daughters take the Father's love into the world. Jesus said:

"As the Father has sent Me, so I am sending you." – John 20:21 NIV

How Sons and Daughters Carry Revival

1. They Walk in the Father's Love

- Sons and daughters bring transformation through love, not judgment.
- They create safe places for the lost and broken to encounter God.

2. They Operate in Supernatural Power

- The Spirit of Sonship releases miracles, signs, and wonders.

- Jesus said: "Freely you have received; freely give." – Matthew 10:8

3. They Shift Atmospheres Wherever They Go

- Sons and daughters bring the Kingdom into workplaces, schools, cities, and nations.
- Revival is not limited to church services—it flows through everyday life.

4. They Raise Up Other Sons and Daughters

- Revival is not about one person—it is about multiplication.
- Sons make disciples, raising up spiritual sons and daughters who carry the fire of revival.

True revival happens when sons and daughters take their place and reveal the Father.

How to Sustain Revival Through a Culture of Sonship

Many revivals have started with great power, but they did not last because they were not built on sonship. Revival that is not rooted in identity and relationship with the Father will fade over time.

"Remain in Me, as I also remain in you... apart from Me, you can do nothing." – John 15:4-5 NKJV

Keys to Sustaining Revival Through Sonship

1. Stay Anchored in the Father's Presence

- Revival is not about events—it is about daily intimacy with the Father.
- "Those who wait on the Lord will renew their strength." – Isaiah 40:31

2. Build a Culture of Sons and Daughters, Not Orphans

- Revival dies when people strive and compete instead of walking in family and unity.
- Sons honor one another and create a culture of love and empowerment.

3. Keep Revival Focused on the Father, Not Just Signs and Wonders

- Miracles are a sign of the Kingdom, but they are not the end goal—knowing the Father is.
- Jesus said: "Many will say to Me, 'Lord, Lord, did we not prophesy in Your name?' But I will say, 'I never knew you.'" – Matthew 7:22-23

4. Pass Revival to the Next Generation

- Revival is not just for today—it must be handed down to future sons and daughters.
- True revival happens when we train and release others to walk in sonship and power.

Sons and daughters carry the fire of revival and ensure that it never dies.

The Time for Revival is Now

Jesus told His disciples: "Do you not say, 'There are still four months until harvest'? I tell you, open your eyes and look at the fields— they are ripe for harvest." – John 4:35 The world is hungry for the love of the Father. It is time for sons and daughters to rise up and bring revival to the nations. The Father is asking:

- Will you carry the fire of revival?
- Will you reveal My love to the world?
- Will you take your place as a son or daughter and bring heaven to earth?

The time is NOW—revival is here, and it starts with the revelation of sonship.

Sons and Daughters Ignite Revival

The Father is saying: "My child, you are called to carry My love and power to the world. The world is waiting for you. Step into revival and reveal My heart." You are not waiting for revival —you are revival. You are not just a participant—you are a carrier of the Father's presence. You are not powerless—you are a son or daughter, filled with the Spirit of God. It's time to step into the greatest revival the world has ever seen.

Activation Prayer

Father, I receive the Spirit of Sonship and the fire of revival. I renounce every orphan mindset and step into my identity as Your child. I declare that I am a carrier of Your presence, love, and power. I will bring revival wherever I go. Use me to ignite a move of God that will transform generations. Amen.

Discussion Questions

1. How does the Father's love—revealed through sonship—shift our understanding of what revival truly is and what it should look like in the Church today?

2. How have you experienced (or witnessed) the orphan mindset in the Church, and what changes when believers begin to walk as sons and daughters instead?

3. What steps can you personally take to carry and sustain revival in your life, home, and community through a culture of intimacy with the Father?

CONCLUSION
GO FORTH AS SONS

You were never meant to live as an orphan.

From the very beginning, before time whispered its first breath, you were dreamt of by a Father whose love has no end. His desire was never just to save you, but to know you, walk with you, transform you, and call you His own. Through every page of this journey, you've been invited out of striving and into belonging. Out of fear and into faith. Out of slavery and into sonship.

Now, it's time to rise.

This book was never just meant to be read—it was meant to be received. You have not simply learned principles. You've been called into a posture. You are not just a student of sonship. You are a son. You are a daughter. You are an heir.

The Spirit of adoption has been whispering truth over your life:

"You are Mine."
"I have not forsaken you."
"I am proud of you."
"I have entrusted you with My Kingdom."

Let those words take root deeper than any wound, louder than any accusation, stronger than any failure. Your past cannot disqualify you. Your weakness cannot intimidate Him. Your questions do not offend Him. He is not looking for perfection—He is looking for those willing to be loved.

And love changes everything.

As a son, you don't have to fight for approval—you live from it. You don't chase affirmation—you carry it. You don't prove your worth—you rest in it. Every battle, every assignment, every act of obedience now flows from a place of inheritance. You're not a servant trying to earn a place at the table. You are a beloved child seated with Christ in heavenly places.

From this day forward, walk in that truth.

Let it shape your prayers. Let it deepen your worship. Let it guard your relationships. Let it empower your leadership. Let it humble your heart and lift your head. Because the world is not waiting for more gifted people—it is groaning for revealed sons and daughters.

Go into your city, your family, your ministry, and your workplace with the authority of Heaven and the tenderness of a child who knows they are loved. When you lead, lead as a son. When you serve, serve as a daughter. When you suffer, suffer as one who is not alone. When you succeed, succeed as one who knows the glory belongs to the Father.

So now, I speak this over you:

> May the Father's embrace be your constant place of rest.
> May the Son's example be the pattern you pursue.
> May the Spirit's voice be the compass that leads you.
> May your identity never be stolen by circumstance.
> May your destiny never be hijacked by fear.
> May you build houses of belonging.
> May you raise up sons and daughters who know who they are.
> And may the Earth be filled with the glory of God through your
> life.

Go forth—not as a slave, not as a stranger, not as an orphan…
But as a son.
As a daughter.
As a carrier of the Kingdom.
As a reflection of the Father.
The world is waiting.

ABOUT THE AUTHOR

Tom Cornell is the Senior Leader of SOZO Church in Washington state, founder of Walk in the Light International and SOZO Network. Tom is married to his beautiful wife Katy and lives in the Puget Sound area with her and their three kids. He has been in ministry pastoring and teaching the body of Christ since 2008.

He has a passion to see the body of Christ moving from people with an orphan mindset to that of sonship; equipping the body to do the work of Jesus resulting in seeing the Kingdom of God manifested here on earth.